The Soviet Union Eastern Europe and the World Food Markets

Eastern European Agriculture
0 Miles 100 200
Grain
Livestock
Main railways
Rostock
Stralsund
Gdynia
Gdansk
Szczecin
Berlin
Warsaw
Prague
Budapest
Bucharest
Constanta
Stalin
Burgas
Sofia
PIGS
POTATOES
SUGAR BEET
WHEAT
RYE
FRUIT
MAIZE
FORESTRY
GRAPES
COTTON
TOBACCO
ESSENTIAL OILS
EAST GERMANY
POLAND
CZECHOSLOVAKIA
HUNGARY
RUMANIA
BULGARIA

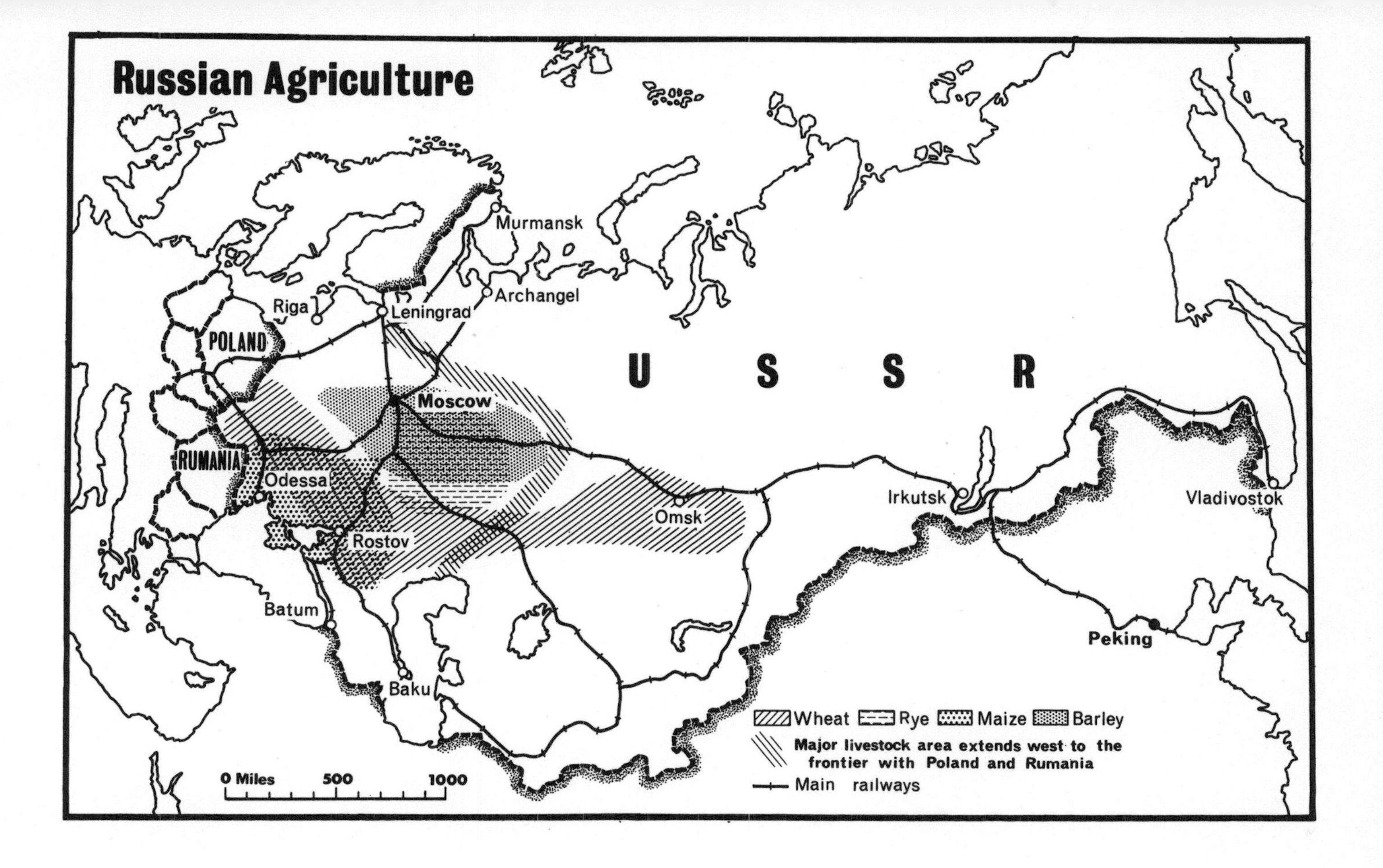
Russian Agriculture
U S S R
Murmansk
Archangel
Riga
Leningrad
POLAND
Moscow
RUMANIA
Odessa
Omsk
Irkutsk
Vladivostok
Rostov
Batum
Baku
Peking
0 Miles 500 1000
Wheat Rye Maize Barley
Major livestock area extends west to the frontier with Poland and Rumania
Main railways

PRAEGER SPECIAL STUDIES IN INTERNATIONAL ECONOMICS

The Soviet Union Eastern Europe and the World Food Markets

JOHN BUTLER
The Economist Intelligence Unit

Prepared by
THE ECONOMIST INTELLIGENCE UNIT *for*
FREDERICK A. PRAEGER, PUBLISHER
New York • London

The purpose of the Praeger Special Studies is to make specialized research monographs in international economics and politics available to the academic, business, and government communities. For further information, write to the Special Projects Division, Frederick A. Praeger, Publisher, 111 Fourth Ave., New York, N. Y. 10003.

FREDERICK A. PRAEGER, *Publisher*
111 Fourth Ave., New York 3, N. Y., U.S.A.
77-79 Charlotte Street, London W.1, England

Published in the United States of America in 1964
by Frederick A. Praeger, Inc., Publisher

Library of Congress Catalog Card Number: 64-16672

Printed in The United States of America

Prefatory Note

The countries covered in this study are the Soviet Union, Bulgaria, Czechoslovakia, East Germany, Hungary, Poland and Rumania.

All quantities are expressed in metric tons, unless otherwise stated.

Population Trends

Population estimates for mid-1961 are shown below:

	million		million
Bulgaria	7.9	Rumania	18.6
Czechoslovakia	13.8	Total Eastern Europe	97.4
East Germany	17.1	U.S.S.R.	218.0
Hungary	10.0		
Poland	30.0	Total Bloc	315.4

Based on an annual growth rate of 0.9 per cent between 1958 and 1970 for the East European countries and of 1.5 per cent for the U.S.S.R. over the same period, population projections for 1969-71 are as follows:

Eastern Europe	108.6	millions
U.S.S.R.	248.6	millions
Total Bloc	357.2	millions

CONTENTS

Introduction

In the past the role of the U.S.S.R. and Eastern Europe in world food markets has been a constantly variable factor capable of swinging the market for a particular commodity from one extreme to another. There is little to suggest that this situation will change in the short term, although over a five to ten year period it is probable that the Soviet Bloc will achieve a more stable position in relation to the world supply and demand balance for major foodstuffs. This, however, will be the consequence more of development within the Soviet Bloc economy of its own resources than a move to a more sophisticated approach to trade in food products.

The present pattern of Soviet Bloc intervention in world markets in temperate foodstuffs is generally carried out regardless of price considerations whether it be the disposal of crops grown in surplus or restocking operations as the result of shortfalls in domestic production. There are a number of fundamental reasons why the Bloc maintains this attitude and fails to use the mechanisms of international commodity trade in an orthodox way:-

i) There is a basic mistrust of the capitalist trade system, which is a natural consequence of Communist ideology, but this seems to be allied to a misunderstanding of how the markets operate. This is revealed clearly in some of the more notorious Eastern Bloc unloading operations, for example, the sale of barley at extremely low prices when it would have been possible to achieve higher earnings if the barley had been offered through a conventional commodity market. In the same way purchases which are made at world prices are never, or rarely, made in small regular quantities which would not disturb the market price level, but are made in enormous quantities at moments when it is clear that stocks in the Bloc are almost exhausted, thus serving to exaggerate price fluctuations. Since purchases are often not even made in one large order, but in a number of relatively big slices, the Bloc not only causes prices to rise but may itself buy some of its requirements at the top of the price cycle. No serious attempts seem to be made to secure any advantageous price position at times of world surplus which a large purchaser might reasonably expect. This suggests that the governments of the Bloc regard world commodity trade in temperate foodstuffs which they themselves grow as an expedient which is only to be used in emergencies and not a reasonable structure which can be used for the buying and selling of goods on a normal commercial basis. In other sectors, the marketing of its consumer durables, of which cars are at present the most important, the East follows extremely orthodox commercial methods of export and sale. This concept, however, is not applied to food except in the case of some of the traditional exports by Poland, Hungary and Rumania of processed foodstuffs.

ii) The Bloc has an abnormally unstable production structure of primary foodstuffs, especially food grains. Over the past ten years it has produced surpluses of some cereals in one year and experienced shortfalls in others, or might have a generally good crop year which could be succeeded by one or two poor years culminating, as in 1963, in an overall failure. This means that the Bloc is not obliged to depend on world markets every year for either imports, as in the case of grain Britain does, or to sell export surpluses which is the traditional US position for wheat. Thus its needs are irregular in the grain sector, and tend to be unpredictable from one crop year to the next, unlike the situation which exists in rubber where the U.S.S.R. is a regular purchaser on the world market, although again not in an orthodox pattern. Hence, it intervenes in the world market only when its own agricultural production fails to meet requirements or when it has an exportable surplus which it needs to turn into hard currency to finance purchases of plant or equipment from the West. Its intervention depends on basic needs which in turn are directly controlled by the volume of food production in the Bloc. This is the fundamental factor governing Soviet policy in international food trade, but production in the Bloc suffers not only from the usual vicissitudes of weather but also from a number of structural failings including planning, which has been extremely ill-directed, a failure to win the cooperation of the peasants, and a rigid and inefficient marketing system. Production is discussed in Chapter I.

iii) Because the Soviet Bloc is short of convertible funds and cannot produce readily marketable goods for sale to the West it suffers from a severe problem of balancing imports against exports. This situation has created a firm attachment to the principle of barter, which is still adhered to despite efforts to encourage a move towards a multilateral payments system. In some respects this is a relic from a period when the East desperately depended on imports of capital equipment to build up its industrial capacity and could pay only in basic commodities which were often already in world surplus. At that time it was also loth to enter world markets for ideological reasons. In the sixties the

East has much more to offer and its need for Western capital goods is far more highly specialised. Nevertheless the habit of dealing by barter dies hard and even in cases where direct barter is impossible trade is conducted on the basis of a series of bilateral agreements firmly tied to the principle of equal value exchanges; in practice this is virtually a barter system. But the barter deal, or its equivalent bilateral trade agreements, has little place in the mechanism of the sophisticated international commodity markets where the principle of monetary transactions is fundamental to the whole pricing structure. Hence dealing through international markets is an alien concept to men who see trade in terms of barter and this goes far to explain the reluctance with which the Communist Bloc uses the world system.

iv) The needs of the population as consumers in the Soviet Bloc are not the mainspring of foreign trade as they tend to be in the West. In the Communist Bloc import needs, or instead under Stalin basic food needs, are subordinate to priorities laid down by the planners, who have in the past always given overwhelming emphasis to industrial growth. For example, most Western European countries are substantial importers of coffee because there is a heavy demand from consumers accustomed to drinking it; in the East, Poland, for example, is a country which traditionally consumes large quantities of coffee, but in fact the state trading organisations import very little coffee mainly because there are few trade agreements with coffee growing countries and because coffee has been given a low priority by the U.S.S.R., which itself is a virtual non-consumer of coffee. Thus demand is not an important factor in influencing import policy except in cases where a real hardship would be incurred by the population which might have political repercussions. So far this is limited to very basic foodstuffs such as grain and cannot be said to apply with much force even to meat.

The results of this attitude in the Communist Bloc are to make it an unpredictable element in world food trade capable of upsetting commodity prices or of bolstering a flagging market. But it also makes for a surprising relationship with primary producing countries. Soviet grain purchases in 1963 were of direct benefit to Canadian wheat growers who saw Russian intervention as a gift from the gods at a time when their earning prospects were dismal. At the same time quite small Soviet re-exports of tropical produce, such as coffee, have caused great concern among the growing countries, generally highly under-developed. Also because demand does not govern import policy, the Bloc buys relatively little from tropical producers, thus making small contribution to the export earnings of, for example, the emerging African countries. Apart from Cuban produce, mainly of course sugar, the Soviet bloc does not offer an outlet to the tropical producers even equivalent to its economic strength quite apart from its political role. Thus for tropical produce the world market structure virtually excludes the Communist Bloc.

For the future it will be necessary to continue to regard the Bloc as a somewhat incalculable factor. In Chapter 4, however, it is suggested that the East will become a less important purchaser of grains and may well eventually rejoin the U.S. as a constant net exporter, with disastrous effects on prices unless the pattern of the market is radically revised. In sugar it seems probable that Cuban production can be excluded from the calculations of future world market supply, hence the market is likely to attract the necessary supplies from elsewhere so that if the regime in Cuba changes, the West might well find it difficult to absorb Cuban production as it was absorbed in the 1950's. For other commodities it is probable that the Eastern Bloc will become a more important purchaser as the standards of living rise and as consumer choice becomes a more potent factor. What is clear is that the Communist Bloc possesses great potential power either to disrupt the structure of the international commodity markets, as in the case of wheat in the mid-seventies perhaps, or to strengthen them, as in the case of coffee.

In the long run it is certain that the Eastern Bloc will acquire a far more sophisticated attitude towards trade in foodstuffs through organised markets. The crucial question will then become that of how the government will use its economic power. While it is possible that a knowledge of the technique of international commodity trade would enable the Communists toactively undermine the present structure set up and operated by capitalists, it will also be true that the East will be dependent on the international trade structure to fulfil its own needs and to sell its own surpluses. Thus a sophisticated appreciation of the system and purpose of world food markets will entail an understanding of the problems of conducting international trade in foodstuffs without a mechanism which is available to all producers and consumers and readily supported by them. Hence it is likely that the Communist Bloc will be more constructive in its policy. At the same time a wheat surplus of its own, which will aggravate the overall world surplus, may well encourage it to seek worldwide commodity agreements which would solve not only Russia's problem but also those of the North American growers. This approach in the temperate sector could well be followed by a spirit of cooperation over the problems of tropical foodstuffs.

The Soviet Union Eastern Europe and the World Food Markets

CHAPTER 1 PRODUCTION OF FOODSTUFFS WITHIN THE BLOC

The relations of the Soviet Bloc with world food markets are almost entirely governed by the pattern of domestic production. In years of good harvests the Communist countries often enter the market as sellers of grains, whereas a crop failure will result in large purchases by the Bloc. Thus the Soviet Bloc trades in foodstuffs only through necessity, either to get rid of surpluses or to make good deficiencies in supplies. Even in the case of commodities such as meat or tea of which the Bloc is always a net importer the primary influence on the level of purchases is domestic production. Since world market price considerations are of negligible importance in prompting sales or purchases of foodstuffs the key to the future is the level of output which can be attained by agriculture. The farm structure in the Soviet Bloc is extremely inefficient in most countries, although in the U.S.S.R. a real effort is now being made to modernise techniques and rationalize planning. The past is strewn with false starts and misdirected policies which have seriously affected not only the absolute volume of production but have also made for low yields and high costs. Allied to this structural weakness in the producing sector of agriculture, the marketing system is far from efficient, with a state organisation being supplemented, and to some extent frustrated, by unofficial private marketing.

OVERALL FOOD PRODUCTION

The production of basic foodstuffs in the Eastern Bloc has long been given first priority in economic planning and despite considerable set-backs the overall growth of food output in the Bloc over the last ten years has been very impressive. For reasons examined more closely below it is extremely difficult to pinpoint the exact volume of food production in the Communist countries, but the following indices may be taken as a fair guide to the rate of progress. The statistics on which they are based represent the official view of actual output.

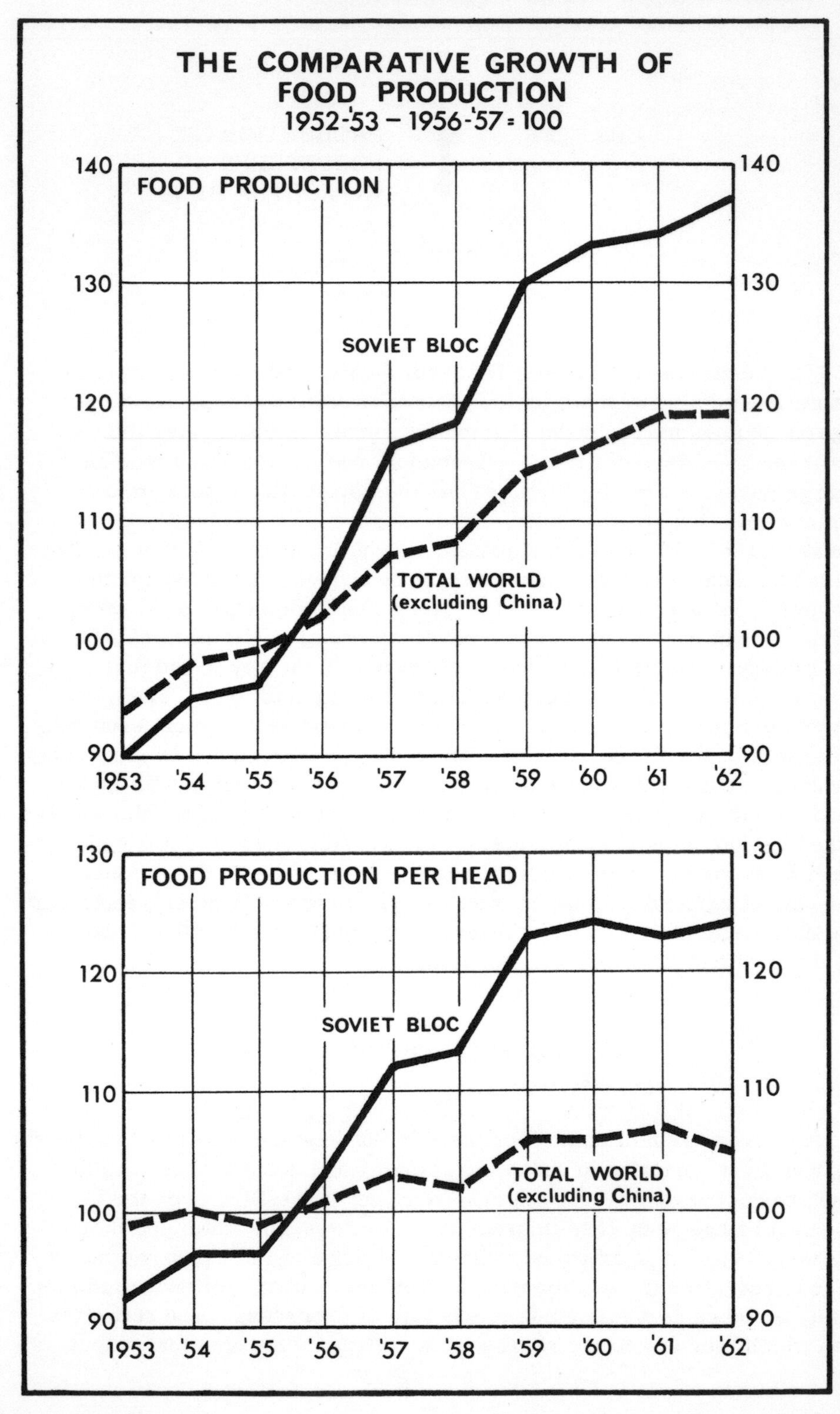
THE COMPARATIVE GROWTH OF FOOD PRODUCTION
1952-'53 – 1956-'57 = 100
FOOD PRODUCTION
SOVIET BLOC
TOTAL WORLD
(excluding China)
140
130
120
110
100
90
1953
'54
'55
'56
'57
'58
'59
'60
'61
'62
FOOD PRODUCTION PER HEAD
SOVIET BLOC
TOTAL WORLD
(excluding China)
130
120
110
100
90
1953
'54
'55
'56
'57
'58
'59
'60
'61
'62

Although this in itself may be suspect, it is reasonable to assume that the growth factor from one year to the next can be taken as roughly conforming to the actual change in the volume of food produced. There are inherent reasons why very good or very poor harvests may be exaggerated, but the broad pattern of growth is fairly reflected.

From the chart opposite it is clear that over the last decade food production in the Soviet Bloc has been expanding at a faster rate than the average pace of the whole world. There is every indication that economic policy will continue to lay heavy emphasis on agriculture even beyond the general limit of the present plans, 1970. The table below showing the broad aims of the Soviet Union's agricultural policy indicates that further strides forward are planned over the next decade and a half.

FOOD OUTPUT IN THE U.S.S.R. 1960-80

Million tons	Actual 1960	1965	Planned 1970	1980
Grain	134	160-178	230	290-310
Meat (deadweight)	9	16	25	30-32
Milk	62	100-105	135	170-180
Eggs (no. '000 million)	27	37	68	110-116
Sugar beet	58	70-78	86	98-108
Potatoes	84	-	140	156
Other vegetables & melons	19	-	47	55
Fruit	5	-	28	51

Sources FAO and national sources.

From this table it can be seen that the Soviet Union plans to double the production of grain between 1960 and 1975; to more than treble meat output by 1980; to almost treble milk output; and to increase potato and sugar beet crops by about 90 per cent. If these targets can be met the position of the U.S.S.R. and the Soviet Bloc as a whole, in relation to world food supplies, will be completely different from that occupied at present.

The actual levels of production of foodstuffs in the Soviet Bloc are given in Appendix 1 p 57 . These are also shown as a percentage of total world output of the same crops in the charts shown below, p. 4 . The figures relate to the period 1958-61 inclusive.

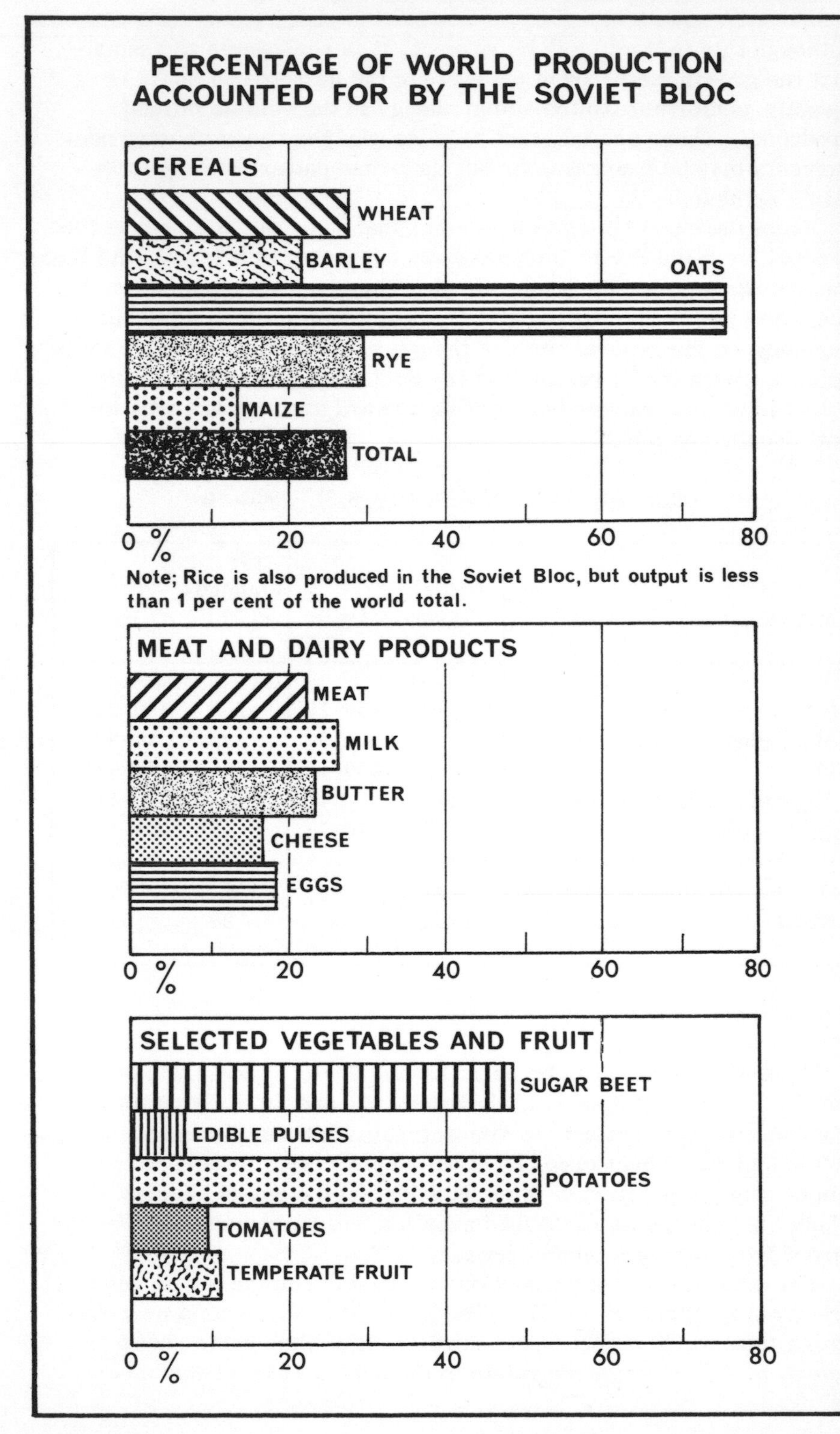
PERCENTAGE OF WORLD PRODUCTION
ACCOUNTED FOR BY THE SOVIET BLOC
CEREALS
WHEAT
BARLEY
OATS
RYE
MAIZE
TOTAL
0 %
20
40
60
80
Note; Rice is also produced in the Soviet Bloc, but output is less than 1 per cent of the world total.
MEAT AND DAIRY PRODUCTS
MEAT
MILK
BUTTER
CHEESE
EGGS
0 %
20
40
60
80
SELECTED VEGETABLES AND FRUIT
SUGAR BEET
EDIBLE PULSES
POTATOES
TOMATOES
TEMPERATE FRUIT
0 %
20
40
60
80

Because agricultural statistics for the Eastern Bloc cannot be taken as accurate, and as the world production figures include a number of approximations for non-reporting countries, the percentage share of world output accounted for by the Eastern Bloc may be subject to error, but the relationship between the different crops shown should be fairly accurately reflected. In terms of population the Soviet Union and the six Communist countries under discussion with 315.4 million estimated in mid-1961 represent almost 15 per cent of the estimated world total. In the period under consideration the Bloc produced 27 per cent of the world total of temperate cereals, including 76 per cent of the total oats grown and 29 per cent of the wheat. The Bloc accounts for nearly a quarter of the recorded meat output, over 25 per cent of milk, nearly a quarter of the world's supply of butter, other than that consumed on farms, and 18 per cent of all eggs. In vegetables the Bloc grows about half of world total of sugar beet and potatoes.

PRODUCTION IN EACH BLOC MEMBER COUNTRY

The U. S. S. R.

FOOD OUTPUT IN THE U. S. S. R.
Mean of the crops 1958-61 (inclusive)
(million tons)

Wheat	61.1	Dairy products	
Maize	17.4	Milk	61.2
Rye	16.4	Butter	0.8
Barley	13.1	Cheese	0.25
Oats	12.0	Eggs (no. '000 million)	25.9
Total cereals	120.0	Sugar beet	51.7
Rice	0.2	Potatoes	85.4
Soya beans	0.2	Edible pulses	1.3
Meat	8.6	Temperate fruit (grapes only)	1.9
Sunflower seed	4.1	Citrus fruit	0.03
		Tea	0.035

Source FAO.

The Soviet Union is the only country in the Bloc in which farming is completely nationalised. The two basic units of the system are the state farm, which is usually a very large-scale operation where the staff and labour are paid a fixed wage, and the collective which resembles a co-operative in that wages are supplemented by a modest share in the profits from selling the crops. The produce of state farms is simply collected directly by a state food storage organisation while that of the collectives is bought at a bulk purchase price. Under this system the collectives have to buy their own equipment while the state farms are supplied by the government. State farms now tend to be used mainly for specialised farming such as high grade cattle breeding, horticulture, viticulture etc, while the production of meat, grain and animal feedstuffs is left to the collectives.

Despite many years of effort the central government has not yet found a satisfactory way in which to exercise a decisive influence on the pattern of agriculture. There is a moderate manipulative effect in the price mechanism applied to bulk purchasing which allows for a price differential according to quality, but this has not proved strong enough an incentive to more efficient farming. At the same time shortages of manpower and equipment prevent the full exploitation of marginal land or the observance of a proper system of crop rotation.

Because of these factors there is a very high loss in agricultural output. This loss is enlarged by the constant difficulties faced in the transport sector and the lack of adequate storage facilities. Another vital element, the human factor, is extremely difficult to assess. It is known that a number of malpractices are indulged in such as selling underweight to the bulk purchasing organisation, pilfering and straight falsification of accounts. It may be safely assumed that the average losses from all causes in food production amount to about 20 per cent of the official output figures.

Over the whole agricultural sector there lies the constant handicap of inefficient operation due to shortages of vital equipment. Although statistically Soviet agriculture is fully mechanised, it is seriously undersupplied with tractors, agricultural machinery and trucks. Even according to official sources some 40 per cent of the country's tractor population is more or less permanently out of commission because of the lack of spares and replacement tyres; the truck fleet is considered to be depleted by about 30 per cent through constant breakdowns. The vehicle shortage is high-lighted by the fact that during the harvest trucks are requisitioned from industry, which sometimes entails journeys of over 1,000 miles. The effect of these accumulated factors on agricultural costs must be extremely high.

The government is well aware of these shortcomings in the agricultural sector. Over the last three years a plan has been in operation which provides for specialisation in the motor industry to provide for a higher output of tractors and other agricultural machinery. In December 1963 following a disastrous harvest the plenary session of the Central Committee of the Communist Party was devoted to the discussion of one item, the speeding up of the development of the chemical industry in the period 1964-70. This was due to the fact that the main part of the shortfall in the grain harvest was attributed to the acute shortage of chemical fertilisers. In the report given to the plenary session by Mr. Khrushchev it was envisaged that the production of chemicals would be increased by 300-350 per cent by 1970; the output of mineral fertilisers is to be stepped up from 20 million tons to 70-80 million tons in 1970. In fact, however, a crash programme to develop the chemical industry may reflect on the level of output of agricultural machinery, by switching some plant from supplying the needs of farm equipment production, to serving the chemical industry.

Public ownership of the land has not eliminated private initiative in food marketing and it is thought that non-state trading accounts for about a fifth of the total turnover in food. Nearly every town or settlement has its private food market where produce is sold at non-controlled prices. The main items traded are bread, cakes, vegetables and dairy products. Supplies come from various sources: collective farms which have fulfilled their production quotas and are selling their surpluses, although this is often a matter of falsifying the returns; collective farm workers selling the produce of their own individual plots; workers in forestry trusts selling berries, mushrooms and game; railwaymen bringing food from areas of surplus to deficiency areas; and black market operators selling stolen food. The importance of these markets is revealed by the fact that no Soviet government has tried to abolish them, although occasionally 'speculators' are arrested and harsh deterrent sentences passed. This system is tolerated because it is a means of supplying the population with an additional quantity of food equal to about a fifth of the bulk purchases made by the state; because it allows collectives and individual agricultural workers to increase their incomes and thus helps to slow the flow of workers leaving the land; and finally, because the price movements of the private market are a useful indication to the government in fixing its bulk purchase prices and subsidies.

Domestic agricultural policy

Since 1945 there has been a slowly widening gap between the production and the consumption of agricultural produce. No attention was paid to the needs of agriculture in the immediate post-war years, as industrial reconstruction and rehabilitation absorbed all the country's resources. Malenkov's policy of stimulating agricultural production by better purchase prices and a greater supply of consumer goods was very well received, but did not last long enough to show any positive results. A number of steps were taken by his successor Khrushchev to alleviate the shortages of food. Some of the collective farms were amalgamated to form larger units; tractor stations were finally disbanded and the equipment distributed among the farms in an effort to secure a better use of it; State supervision was improved; the planning of agricultural production was decentralised in order to achieve a greater elasticity; and a detailed system of accountancy was introduced on the farms. None of these policies was successful, however, as they failed to tackle the major problems of the shortages of manpower, equipment and fertilisers and the lack of good husbandry.

The major steps taken by Mr Khrushchev were:-

1. Maize production. In order to overcome the shortage of animal fodder, a substantial part of Russian agricultural resources was shifted to the cultivation of maize. This policy failed because of the shortage of specialized equipment and the lack of experience in large-scale cultivation of new crops. It also caused a considerable drop in the cultivation of other crops because of the shift of labour and equipment.

2. Virgin lands. The policy of opening up new virgin lands failed completely as no appreciable surplus of grain has ever been obtained from these areas. At the same time the agricultural areas in Western Russia were deprived of their best young farmers who "volunteered" for work in the virgin lands.

3. The reorganisation of the automotive industries in order to achieve a greater production of agricultural equipment. This was carried out during the current Seven Year Plan, and was the first major effort to solve the problem of mechanisation of agriculture. The tractor and agricultural machinery factories are now being re-equipped and expanded and a large part of the engineering industry, including shipyards, has been converted to the production of spares and the assembly of agricultural equipment. At the same time the synthetic rubber and tyre industries are being developed in order to overcome the acute lack of tyres.

4. The plan for the development of the agro-chemical industries. This is, however, clashing with the plan for the production of agricultural equipment. In order to produce the chemical

engineering equipment needed for the construction of fertiliser and pesticide plants, part of the engineering industry, which has been working for the automotive industries, will have to be reconverted to the production of chemical equipment. This will mean a slower rate of production in the tractor and agricultural machinery sector.

The Future

At present Soviet agriculture suffers from a shortage of mechanical equipment. At the same time it is very vulnerable to adverse weather conditions because of the lack of adequate transport facilities, and the shortage of storage capacity. In addition soil exhaustion in a number of areas, due to the scarcity of chemical fertilisers, aggravates the whole problem. To remedy this situation the government is devoting its energies to rapid increases in the manufacture of agricultural equipment and to great advances in the chemical industry. Both of these moves will be slow and painful and it will take at least three years before any real effect can be felt. During this time the Soviet economy will be subject to extremely heavy pressures. Agricultural output will expand because of the increase in the flow of equipment and fertilisers, but not to the extent planned by the government, i.e. sufficiently to close the gap between supply and average annual consumption. If the U.S.S.R. is fortunate enough to have three bumper harvests consecutively, it may be able to dispense with large-scale food imports, but only one bad harvest is needed to compel the government to buy extensively from abroad, at the cost of depleting the gold reserves that are badly needed for the import of capital goods from the West (see p.44).

Eastern Europe

Although the pattern of agriculture in Eastern Europe is very diverse it can be safely said that the standard of land cultivation and animal husbandry is higher than in the Soviet Union, with the exception of some regions of Bulgaria and Rumania, and the whole of Albania, which is not covered in this study. State ownership of land is not so widespread as in the Soviet Union. On the whole, the use of mechanised aids is more extensive and more efficient than in Russia, and better transport and storage facilities are available. Almost every country has well developed canning and food processing industries, often geared to exporting. In at least two Bloc countries, Poland and Rumania, over half of total food production is accounted for by non-state-owned farms.

A division can be made between the agricultural countries,

Hungary, Rumania and Bulgaria, and the industrial countries, East Germany, Czechoslovakia and Poland, which have to supplement their own food production with substantial imports. The agricultural countries almost invariably produce agricultural surpluses which are exported to other Bloc countries and to outside countries. Although the industrial members of the Bloc import large quantities of grain and fodder, they also export specialised food products to the West to earn convertible currency. The inter-Bloc export of food is made more difficult by the practice of payment in kind, usually capital goods, deliveries of which are invariably delayed, and sometimes delivered below standard.

The production patterns of the individual Bloc countries are given below.

Bulgaria

FOOD OUTPUT IN BULGARIA
Mean of the crops 1958-61 (inclusive)
(million tons)

Wheat	2.29	Dairy products	
Maize	1.08	Milk	1.08
Barley	0.56	Cheese	0.07
Oats	0.20	Eggs (no. '000 million)	1.10
Rye	0.09	Sugar beet	1.36
Total cereals	4.22	Potatoes	0.40
		Onions	0.11
Rice	0.04	Edible pulses	0.10
Meat	0.30	Tomatoes	0.58
Sunflower	0.29	Fruit	1.39

Source FAO.

The land is best suited for livestock breeding and horticulture. Soviet political pressure is strongest here and Moscow has consistently pressed Bulgaria to develop its meat and vegetable potential to meet the needs of the rest of the Bloc. Currently Bulgaria is the largest meat exporter to the U.S.S.R. and supplies vegetables to Russia, Czechoslovakia and East Germany. Food production, however, suffers from a shortage of agricultural labour. In an attempt to overcome this the government is merging collective farms into larger units and introducing specialisation, e.g. cattle ranching.

Officially land is 100 per cent nationalised but in fact only the larger farms are proper state farms; for the rest the system is a mixture of collectives some of which are disguised family farms. The farming population is burdened with additional duties such as the building and maintaining of roads, and land reclamation which exacerbate the shortage of labour. The area of marginal land which could be put to agricultural purposes is small as heavy encroachments have been made by various industrial projects.

It is probable that about 90 per cent of total food production is retailed through the state distributing organisations; the activities of the free markets are strictly controlled and the range of produce they have to offer is somewhat limited. Despite its agricultural status there are frequent shortages of food in Bulgaria.

The main exports are vegetables, fresh and canned, to the U.S.S.R. Czechoslovakia, and East Germany; canned vegetables are also sold to Italy, France, Britain and West Germany.

Czechoslovakia

FOOD OUTPUT IN CZECHOSLOVAKIA
Mean of the crops 1958-61 (inclusive)
(million tons)

Wheat	1.54	Butter	0.06
Barley	1.50	Cheese	0.08
Rye	0.95	Eggs (no. '000 million)	2.21
Oats	0.95	Sugar beet	6.24
Maize	0.50	Potatoes	5.84
Total cereals	5.44	Onions	0.06
		Edible pulses	0.03
Meat	0.44	Tomatoes	0.05
Dairy products		Fruit	0.67
Milk	4.07		

Source FAO.

The main crops are root vegetables, potatoes and sugar beet, cereals and a limited quantity of dairy produce. Land nationalisation is almost completed but there are many outcrops of private ownership, especially among the smaller holdings. Farms are organised into four grades of collectives; the first grade is equivalent to Soviet collective farms, while the fourth is a loose association of small farms, a number of which are still in private hands. There is a tendency for labour to avoid working on the first grade collectives where state supervision is at its most severe. At the same time there is an acute shortage of labour, and the average age of agricultural workers is over 40; all attempts to redirect labour to the land have so far been unsuccessful. Production costs are high, partly because many farms are over-equipped, and labour is short. There is some marginal land in Slovakia available for expansion but it is unlikely to be utilised in view of the problem of the drift off the land. Marketing of foodstuffs is almost exclusively through a state retail organisation, but a very restricted form of private market does exist. There is also a fairly widespread black market which is a constant source of worry to the government.

Czechoslovakia's main exports of agricultural produce are of processed foods such as canned sausages to Western Europe and the U.S., and beer to all markets; hops are also exported to the West.

East Germany

FOOD OUTPUT IN EAST GERMANY
Mean of the crops 1958-61 (inclusive)
(million tons)

Rye	2.03	Butter	0.17
Wheat	1.31	Cheese	0.04
Barley	1.05	Eggs (no. '000 million)	3.32
Oats	0.99	Sugar beet	5.79
Total cereals	5.48	Potatoes	11.80
		Edible pulses	0.06
Meat	2.41	Fruit	0.72
Dairy products			
Milk	6.00		

Source FAO.

The main crops are root vegetables, of which potatoes are the largest single product, and cereals, of which rye is the most important; there is also a fairly large dairy sector. Land nationalisation is now fully complete and no form of private holding is allowed; the final stages of the state take-over process were particularly harshly executed and the morale of agricultural workers had not recovered by the end of 1963. Production is organised on the collective system of which there are three categories, all operating under very close government supervision. There is a severe shortage of labour on the land which the government has tried to remedy by official measures forbidding movement from the country to the towns. Production costs are probably very high since official policy is tending to force farms to operate at the point of diminishing returns.

Marketing of farm produce is strictly supervised by the government and no private markets are known to be in existence. Deliveries to retailers are rationed and fixed prices are maintained, but because of serious shortages the population is obliged to supplement supplies by buying very expensive imported tinned foods. Domestic production is estimated to account for no more than 60 per cent of East Germany's total food requirements.

The main export is sugar, which is sold to West Germany; this is refined from domestically grown beet.

Hungary

FOOD OUTPUT IN HUNGARY
Mean of the crops 1958-61 (inclusive)
(million tons)

Maize	3.15	Dairy products	
Wheat	1.77	Milk	1.95
Barley	0.95	Butter	0.02
Rye	0.37	Cheese	0.02
Oats	0.20	Eggs (no. '000 million)	1.84
Total cereals	6.44	Sugar beet	2.62
		Potatoes	2.21
Rice	0.06	Onions	0.07
Meat	0.5	Edible pulses	0.07
Sunflower seed	0.9	Tomatoes	0.19
		Fruit	1.29

Source FAO

The main crops are cereals and vegetables; animal husbandry is also of great importance as Hungary is the Bloc's largest producer of poultry and, with Rumania, the biggest cattle breeding country; it is also a leading pig supplier, together with Rumania and Czechoslovakia. Land ownership represents a mixture of capitalism and socialism; farmers joining in collectives retain the ownership of their land and livestock, which are used by the collectives acting as the agents of the farmers. Each farmer also withholds a small part of his former land as a private plot. Collectives are the only form of production units and they are very short of equipment because of the speed at which the final stages of land nationalisation were carried out, while as yet they are badly organised and run. Because of this structural weakness the government was still, in 1963 and 1964, encouraging farmers to cultivate their private plots, in order to achieve some quick increases in production without the need for large capital investment. There is a shortage of younger agricultural workers but the industrial reorganisation in 1963 released a number of workers to the land. Production costs are still relatively low but will inevitably rise as most of the collectives need re-equipping; the present shortage of mechanised equipment, farm buildings and fertilisers makes it difficult to raise output to the levels required. But, with the acquisition of the skill to administer large production units efficiently, more equipment and proper incentives, the Hungarian farmer should find a satisfactory modus vivendi within the planned economy and consequently increase the output of foodstuffs.

Private markets are flourishing and enjoy official recognition. It is likely that they account for 80 per cent of the supply of all vegetables, 90 per cent of all fruit and 25 per cent of the pork consumed. State distribution is limited to grain, meat, and imported foods. Free market prices are high but overall these tend to be counterbalanced by the low fixed prices of food distributed by official shops.

The main exports are poultry meat, sold mainly to West Germany and France, and wine which is exported to world markets.

Poland

Poland, together with Hungary and Rumania, is one of the largest producers of wheat and rye, while it is one of the major sheep and pig breeding countries. Dairy produce and potatoes are also important. Poland is the only member of the Bloc to have reversed the trend to land nationalisation, so that by the end of 1963 some 80 per cent of total food produced was grown by private farmers. Private farmers are encouraged to join the Agricultural Circles, which are loosely knit co-operatives formed with the main purpose of joint ownership of equipment such as combines and tractors. A number of state farms are still in operation. Labour is available since in 1963 there was a recession in industry and earnings were better on the land; this has reversed the shift from the country to the towns. Farming is hampered by the shortage of farm buildings, the lack of modern equipment, the high cost of tractors and fuels, and the shortages of fodder and fertilisers. The general scarcity of consumer goods in the shops also acts as a disincentive to greater efforts by the farmers. Production costs fell after the reversion of the bulk of land holdings to private hands but the need to stimulate output has called for a higher rate of investment which is reflected in ex-farm prices.

FOOD OUTPUT IN POLAND
Mean of the crops 1958-61 (inclusive)
(million tons)

Rye	8.42	Butter	0.17
Wheat	2.44	Cheese	0.15
Oats	1.72	Eggs (no. '000 million)	21.41
Barley	1.23	Sugar beet	9.05
Maize	0.03	Potatoes	38.39
Total cereals	13.84	Onions	0.19
		Edible pulses	0.06
Meat	1.78	Tomatoes	0.20
Dairy products		Fruit	0.71
Milk	12.36		

Source FAO.

Food is marketed under a bulk purchase system based on contractual prices according to grade, which are circumscribed by close definition. This method encourages farmers to retain the lower grades of produce for their own consumption and only to market the better quality. Members of agricultural circles benefit from better credit facilities than do private farmers and often qualify for advances. Nevertheless private food markets are very active and handle at least 25 per cent of total food grown. The state distribution system suffers from inefficiencies which occasionally lead to food shortages. Prices on the private market fluctuate sharply.

The main exports are processed foodstuffs and bacon to Britain; prepared meats and canned sausages to Britain and the U.S.; butter to Western Europe; mushrooms and pickles to Western Europe and Israel; and vodka and other spirits to Western Europe and the U.S.

Rumania

Rumania, with the richest soil in Eastern Europe, has the best balanced agricultural economy in the Bloc. Rumania, with Hungary, is the largest producer of maize and rice, and with Poland as well these countries lead in growing wheat and rye. With Bulgaria, Rumania is the main source of vegetables. It is the only supplier of hybrid maize seeds. Cattle and sheep are also bred on an extensive scale. Rumania has rapidly developing fertiliser and tractor industries which have done much to aid the expansion of agricultural production. The exact pattern of land tenure has never been revealed in full but it is clear that private and state ownership exist side by side. On paper the system pretends to be 100 per cent nationalised but it is accepted that a great proportion of smaller collectives exist only on paper. It is also understood that private farmers receive help from nearby collectives. The main system seems to be that small farms close to a collective are given the legal status of collectives but, apart from being paid for the sale of their produce through the collective, remain completely independent. The collectives, however, enter into various arrangements with private farms such as lending them machinery or letting them hire additional labour. There are no indications of a shortage of agricultural labour despite a considerable drift from the land into factories. Rural morale is high because of the reasonable way in which land nationalisation has actually been carried out.

FOOD OUTPUT IN RUMANIA
Mean of the crops 1958-61 (inclusive)
(million tons)

Maize	5.1	Dairy products	
Wheat	3.6	Milk	2.7
Barley	0.4	Butter	0.01
Oats	0.28	Cheese	0.04
Rye	0.11	Eggs (no. '000 million)	2.3
Total cereals	9.49	Sugar beet	2.9
		Potatoes	2.9
Rice	0.04	Onions	0.21
Meat	0.9	Edible pulses	0.19
Sunflower seed	0.45	Tomatoes	0.37
		Fruit	1.7

Source FAO.

Private markets are well developed, selling not only all forms of farm produce but also processed foods such as cakes, butter and cheese. The state food retailing organisations appear to be principally concerned with supplies to the larger towns and industrial centres and seem ready to leave the rest to private enterprise.

Rumania is an exporter of wheat and rye to the Soviet Union, Poland, East Germany and Czechoslovakia, and of maize and tinned meat to the latter two Bloc members.

CHAPTER 2 CONSUMPTION OF FOODSTUFFS

DEMAND AND CONSUMPTION

In Western society consumption of foodstuffs is generally equal to demand. If there is an imbalance between demand and consumption it is the result of supply shortages. In the Communist Bloc demand is of negligible importance in influencing the supply of foodstuffs. Demand becomes an important factor only when supply in a given year falls so far below the level of the previous year that a serious unconcealable shortage exists which could result in political manifestations, e.g. bread riots. Thus consumption can be assessed only in terms of availability; what is made available will be consumed. What is important is what the government chooses to make available to the public. In the last few years the Russian government has become more sensitive to the pressures of public opinion if only because Mr Khrushchev is far less secure than Stalin and hence must attempt to match his promises of higher living standards by his performance in supplying more goods in the shops and at least not permitting food supplies to fall below an accustomed level.

A consumption pattern can be built up only on the basis of average supplies over recent years since it can be assumed that the government will seek to improve on past performances. In the case of bread-grains this now seems to be an article of faith since shortages in domestic production are mitigated by imports. For meat, however, it is extremely unlikely that the great drop in the number of pigs kept in 1963, which was reflected in a meat shortage in the U.S.S.R. and most Eastern European countries, was balanced by equivalent meat imports. Thus at present the emphasis is on consumption of staple foods such as grains, and potatoes, and high protein foods are not yet regarded as essential constituents of diet. Nevertheless Mr Khrushchev has promised the Soviet people that more meat and fats will be available as part of the overall improvement in living standards so that it is probably only a matter of time before meat comes to be regarded as equally important as grains and potatoes in the government's order of priorities for supply. When this occurs it will be true that in a negative sense a minimum demand situation will exist.

The balance of consumption in the Bloc is still heavily in favour of bread and potatoes rather than high protein foods and fruit. Because of supply difficulties it will doubtless be slow to change but, if living standards are to improve, change is inevitable. The pace of change will depend on the attitude of the government in granting priorities to imports of high protein foods to supplement domestic production, and this may be the consequence of political rather than economic decisions. Sugar became an important part of the Soviet diet in 1960 because Cuban sugar became available at a time of shortages in the U.S.S.R. of both bread and meat shortly after Mr Khrushchev had held out prospects of more food in the shops. Consequently the supply of Cuban sugar made if possible to offer greater quantities of one foodstuff to the public as some compensation for the lack of others. If the level of consumption can be taken as creating a minimum level of demand, it may be said that sugar is now in demand and it would be an embarrassment to the Soviet government to let supplies fall much below the 63 kg consumed per head in 1961 (see also p. 49).

Changes in diet of a fairly radical nature have begun, but are extremely insignificant in relation to consumption in the Bloc as a whole. In the U.S.S.R., for example, a few coffee bars have opened and are finding favour with the young, but this phenomenon is confined to Moscow and cannot be regarded as making any impact on the massive consumption of tea in Russia. Reports indicate that wheat is being substituted in the U.S.S.R. for rye in bread making although it will be years before black bread can be expected to disappear.

One of the major breakthroughs in consumption which has still to be made in the supply of coffee to Eastern European countries in sufficient quantities for it again to become the major beverage. The example of the coffee shortage in these countries amply demonstrates the failure of demand to affect supply in the Communist Bloc. But if the trend towards better living conditions continues then it is clear that not only meat and fruit will be supplied in larger quantities, but, eventually, also coffee. When this happens the Bloc will come to rely upon tropical producers as exclusive suppliers of a major requirement for the first time (see p.53).

CONSUMPTION BY COUNTRY

The peoples of the Soviet Bloc are generally heavy consumers of cereals, meat and animal fats. The traditional foods are still eaten in the towns and industrial centres as well as in the country. The Soviet Union is the heaviest consumer of beef, rye, millet and animal fats, while East Germany, Czechoslovakia and Poland lead in the consumption of pork, veal, potatoes and wheat. Pork and poultry both play a prominent role in the diet of Hungary; maize is the principal cereal consumed in Rumania, and lamb and mutton comprise the main meat of Bulgaria.

The consumption by each member country of the Bloc of main foodstuffs is given below. The basis is production and trade in 1961 adjusted for major discrepancies when compared with earlier years.

U.S.S.R.

Million tons

Cereals		Dairy products	
Wheat	62.3	Milk	62.6
Maize	23.9	Butter	0.8
Rye	15.6	Cheese	0.3
Barley	12.3	Eggs (no. '000 million)	29.5
Oats	8.7		
Total cereals	122.8	Sugar	8.0[b]
Rice	0.5[a]	Potatoes	84.3
Soya beans	2.4	Edible pulses	2.2
Meat	9.3	Temperate fruit	2.4
Tropical produce ('000 tons)			
Coffee	24[c]	Citrus fruit	131
Cocoa beans	16	Bananas	22
Tea	59	Raisins	11
		Dates	25

a. Adjusted. b. The actual figures are

1959	1960	1961
6.1	8.3	9.3

c. Only 4,000 tons in 1958 before Russia was committed to imports under trade agreements, and much of this is probably exported to other Bloc countries.

In the U.S.S.R. the availability of cereals is 563 kg per head, although nothing like this amount is actually available for human consumption; an unknown quantity is used as animal feedstuff, seed and for other non-food purposes. Also milling will give only some 72 tons of flour per 100 tons of wheat milled. Thus this figure cannot be related directly to the diet of the population, but it is useful as a guide to grain requirements for all purposes each year. Rice is excluded from the cereal calculation and shown separately. 43 kg per head of meat were made available by official suppliers in 1961. This can be compared with the figure for the U.S. in 1961 which was 96 kg per head.

For a direct comparison it is necessary to make some allowance for the private markets which operate in Russia; on the basis of including this additional source the actual per caput supply of meat to Russians is likely to have amounted to between 47 and 54 kg in 1961. Butter consumption was 3.67 kg per head. Egg production, plus imports, for all purposes amounted to 135 per head, but actual gross consumption could well have reached 150-160 eggs per head; the equivalent U.S. figure was 295 in 1961. Potato consumption amounted to 387 kg per head on official returns, which could in reality well be as high as 450 kg; this total includes potatoes consumed for non-food purposes. Citrus fruit was grown and imported at the rate of 0.6 kg per head per annum.

Bulgaria

'000 tons

Cereals		Dairy products	
Wheat	2,480[a]	Milk	1,190
Maize	1,380	Butter	9
Barley	680	Cheese	90
Oats	210	Eggs (no. million)	840
Rye	70	Sugar	240
Total cereals	4,820	Potatoes	400[a]
Rice	40	Edible pulses	70[a]
Meat	300	Temperate fruit	1,170
Tropical produce			
Cocoa beans	1	Citrus fruit	3

a. Adjusted.

From the table above the supply of cereals per head is 610 kg gross, including animal feedstuffs, seed and other non-food usage. 38 kg of meat are made available from official sources; it is probable that private markets would raise this to 40 kg. Butter consumption on official returns is only 1.14 kg per head, but this may well be nearer 3 kg. 106 eggs were supplied per head of population to meet all requirements, although the actual consumption might well have been closer to 120. Sugar consumption amounted to 30 kg per head in 1961, or less than half the 63 kg supplied to the Soviet population as a result of commitments to Cuba. Potato consumption was some 51 kg per head, while temperate fruit was probably supplied at the rate of 160 kg if the contribution of the private market is included; the equivalent figure for ctirus fruit was 0.38 kg.

Czechoslovakia

'000 tons

Cereals		Dairy products	
Wheat	3,000[a]	Milk	4,160
Barley	1,670	Butter	85
Rye	1,180	Cheese	80
Oats	960	Eggs (no. million)	2,270
Maize	580	Sugar	360[a]
Total cereals	7,390	Potatoes	5,470
Rice	163	Edible pulses	48
Meat	530	Temperate fruit	584
Tropical produce			
Coffee	14	Citrus fruit	38
Cocoa beans	15	Bananas	3

a. Adjusted.

The total availability of cereals amounts to 536 kg per head, including all animal and other non-food uses; rice imports amount to almost 12 kg per head. 38 kg of meat both prepared and fresh were supplied per head by official sources, although an unknown additional quantity may be sold on the black market. Butter was supplied at the rate of 6.1 kg per person, and more was probably available illegally. 164 eggs per person were supplied to meet all needs; a further contribution is probably made by the black market. Sugar consumption was 26 kg per head, averaged over the period 1959-61. Potatoes supplied from official sources amounted to 396 kg per head; temperate fruit to 42 kg; and citrus to 2.75 kg.

The supply of cereals per head of population in East Germany reached 433 kg in the period 1959-61, of which rye accounted for almost a third. The meat supply per head amounted to 155 kg in 1961 and of butter to 13.4 kgs. The number of eggs available was 212 per person. Sugar consumption amounted to 25 kg per head, which is somewhat low for a producing country that also exports to West Germany. 699 kg of potatoes were supplied per head, 48 kg of temperate fruit and 1.46 kg of citrus fruit. Imports of coffee were equivalent to 1.28 kg per head in 1961. There is pressure on the East German government to raise living standards because of the situation of Berlin as a shop-window of the West but so far this has not markedly affected the consumption pattern.

East Germany

'000 tons

Cereals		Dairy produce	
Wheat	2,650[a]	Milk	6,000[a]
Rye	2,300[a]	Butter	230
Barley	1,200[a]	Cheese	60
Oats	1,000	Eggs (no. million)	3,620
Maize	250	Sugar	425
Total cerals	7,400	Potatoes	11,950[a]
Meat	2,650	Edible pulses	70
		Temperate fruit	820
Tropical produce			
Coffee	22	Citrus fruit	25
Cocoa beans	13		

a. Adjusted.

Hungary

'000 tons

Cereals		Dairy produce	
Maize	3,250[a]	Milk	1,950[a]
Wheat	2,350	Butter	9
Barley	1,020[a]	Cheese	11
Rye	340[a]	Eggs (no. million)	
Oats	200[a]		1,770
Total cereals	7,160	Sugar	320[a]
Wheat flour	17	Potatoes	2,075[a]
Rice	57	Edible pulses	44
Soya beans	47[a]	Temperate fruit	1,430
Meat	577	Tomatoes	200
Tropical produce			
Citrus fruit	18		

a. Adjusted.

The availability of cereals per head, excluding imported wheat flour, amounted to some 716 kg, and of rice to 5.7 kg. Almost 58 kg of meat were supplied per caput in 1961 by official sources but it is possible that this was raised to 65-70 kg through the private market. Although official returns suggest that only 0.9 kg of butter are consumed per head, it is probable that private sources supply enough to give a consumption figure nearer to 9 kg. Again, per caput egg supply is almost certainly higher than 177 eggs, even though this is above the Bloc average. Sugar supplies per head amount to 32 kg, potatoes to 207.5 kg, which is also doubtless augmented from unofficial suppliers. fruit consumption is taken to be higher than the 143 kg shown since a great volume of fruit reaches the consumer without being recorded in any official form; the official return will tend to cover the fruit used for jam making and other processed food uses. 1.8 kg per head of citrus fruit is imported annually.

Poland

'000 tons

Cereals		Dairy produce	
Rye	8,670	Milk	12,760
Wheat	4,530	Butter	140
Oats	2,940	Cheese	186
Barley	1,550	Eggs (no. million)	4,700
Maize	84		
Total cereals	17,774	Sugar	1,900
Wheat flour	14	Potatoes	45,040
Rice	85[a]	Edible pulses	50
Soya beans	38[a]	Temperate fruit	620
Meat	1,740	Tomatoes	200
Tropical produce			
Cocoa beans	10	Citrus fruit	36

a. Adjusted.

The total grain supply amounts to 593 kg per head but almost half is accounted for by rye. Although rye produces a higher volume of flour per ton of grain than wheat. Rye flour has neither the food value nor the range of use of wheat flour. Also with a large bacon and ham industry the quantity of grains used as animal feedstuffs is proportionately higher than in other Bloc countries. Consumption of rice is 2.8 kg per head, and of meat of all types, 58 kg. The official returns would suggest a butter consumption of 4.7 kg per head but the actual figure, bolstered by supplies sold on the private market and consumed direct on the farms, is likely to be closer to 6 kg. The supply of eggs per head was 157, and of sugar 63 kg. According to official production figures and export returns 1.5 tons of potatoes per head were available in 1961. 6.6 kg of tomatoes and 20.7 kg of temperate fruit were offered through official suppliers, but doubtless additional quantities reached consumers by way of the private markets; citrus fruit consumption was 1.2 kg per head.

Rumania

'000 tons

Cereals		Dairy produce	
Maize	5,120	Milk	3,040
Wheat	3,980	Butter	13
Barley	470	Cheese	40
Oats	280	Eggs (no. million)	2,520
Rye	60		
Total cereals	9,910	Sugar	283
Rice	50[a]	Potatoes	2,900
Meat	1,050	Edible pulses	240
		Temperate fruit	1,590
Tropical produce		Tomatoes	400
Citrus fruit	13		

a. Adjusted.

The cereal supply in Rumania totals 532.7 kg per head, which is almost as high as that of Poland and is well ahead of that in other Bloc countries. Rice consumption amounted to 2.7 kg per head of population and of meat to 56 kg. On the basis of the official returns butter is supplied at the rate of only 0.7 kg per head, but it is likely that the private market contributes as much as a further 4-5 kg. 135 eggs per person were supplied in 1961 but this too may well have been augmented by the private market which flourishes in Rumania. 156 kg of potatoes were recorded as being supplied per head in 1961. Sugar consumption was 15 kg. Pulse consumption, at an official level of 13 kg per head, is relatively high. The official figure of an overall fruit consumption of 85 kg per head is rather low and it is highly probable that a significant proportion of the fruit bought by individual consumers is supplied by private growers. Tomato consumption is 21.5 kg per head and that of citrus fruit 0.7 kg.

THE OVERALL PATTERN

Consumption of foodstuffs in the Soviet Union and Eastern European countries has reached a stage where a reasonable diet is available for all citizens but because of shortages, not only of high protein foods but also at times of bread-grains and vegetables, the best fed sector of the population is still the farmer or collective farm-worker. The shortages are felt most severely in the urban centres. There is as yet no question of substituting a higher consumption of meat and fats for starchy foods since supplies are barely adequate to provide meat as a supplement to bread and potatoes. Luxury foods are extremely scarce, although some are produced for export to the West. The first priorities in the Eastern Bloc are to produce more food domestically, especially high protein foods, so that the shortages can be ended, and to ensure that the marketing system will be efficient enough to distribute foodstuffs evenly to all sectors of the population. If these objectives can be achieved the role of the private market will certainly diminish in most Bloc countries, although it is too much to expect that it will disappear entirely. When shortages are eventually eliminated consumption should remain roughly stable on a per head basis, and a form of demand will exist. At this point the Bloc will tend to intervene far more frequently in world food markets for the purpose of satisfying domestic demand.

CHAPTER 3 IMPORTS AND EXPORTS

THE PATTERN OF TRADE

Full details of the foreign trade position in foodstuffs are given in Appendix II, p. 65.

Trade with the outside world and inter-bloc exchanges in food products show very sharp annual variations mainly because sales and purchases are geared to the level of production within the Bloc. For this reason the most marked fluctuations from one year to the next are in temperate products of which grain is the most important. The small quantities of tropical produce imported tend to be fairly stable, varying only with political events. The Cuban revolution, for example, completely reversed the previous trend in Bloc trade in sugar. A major political upheaval in a country growing only cocoa beans could well quadruple total imports overnight. However, in the light of known shortfalls and surpluses in domestic agricultural output it is possible to discern a rudimentary trade pattern which is aimed at satisfying certain minimum supply requirements that are almost entirely confined to temperate foodstuffs which are grown in the Bloc.

The Soviet Bloc is generally a net exporter of cereals, vegetables, eggs and butter, canned and prepared meats. It is a net importer of tropical produce, including tea and rice both of which are grown in the Bloc, fresh meat and live cattle, dried milk, wheat flour and, since the Cuban revolution, sugar. In fact, however, the position is far from static and there are constant variations within the different categories. In the case of temperate cereals the annual fluctuations are illustrated below on p. 28. Although the Bloc was a net exporter of cereals in each of the years cited no single cereal was grown every year in quantities sufficient to allow an exportable surplus. The Bloc was a net exporter of wheat in each year except 1961, while there was a net exportable surplus of rye and oats in three out of the four years; for barley the Bloc was a net importer every year except 1961, and for maize exports exceeded imports for two years. In fact this pattern reflects the influence of climate, allied to policy failures, on the production of wheat and other main cereals in the Bloc.

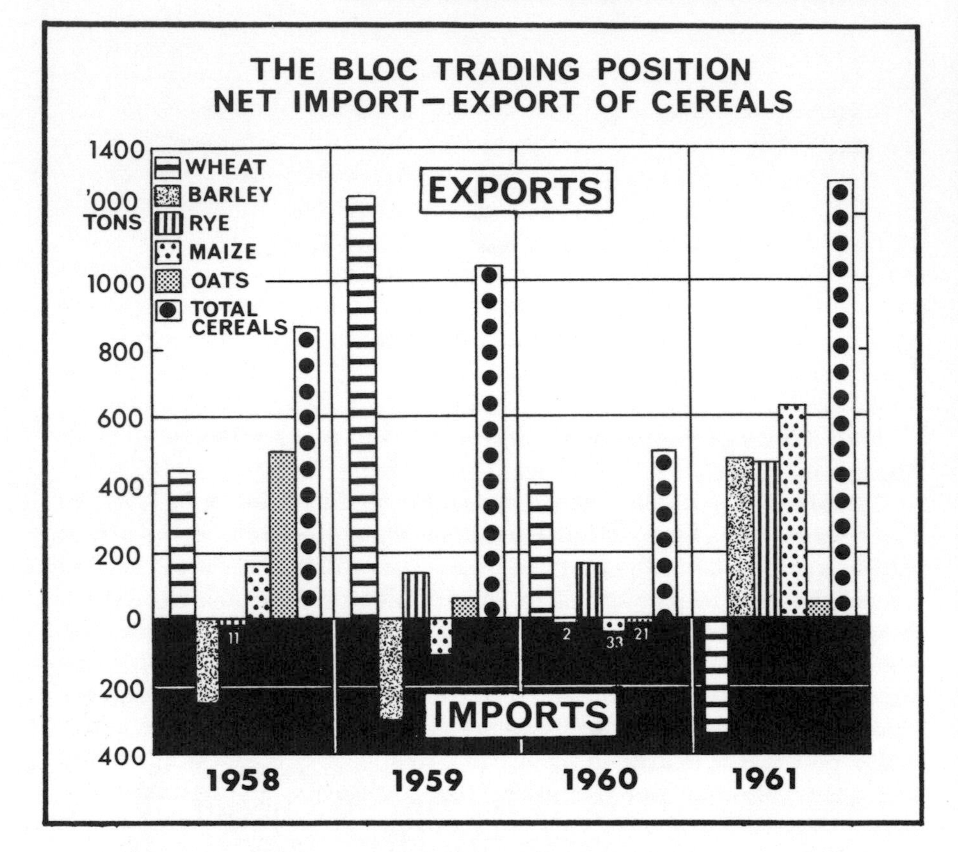

For other produce the position is far less variable. The Bloc is a constant net importer of fresh meat, although ultimately it aims at self-sufficiency; already the Bloc is a net exporter of prepared and canned meat although this is somewhat artificial, since the member countries themselves could well absorb the total prepared and canned meat output of Poland, Czechoslovakia and the Soviet Union, and indeed the imports of this product by the U.S.S.R. far exceed its exports. Exports, however, are maintained in order to earn hard currencies; sales are almost exclusively to the U.S., Britain and West Germany.

In dairy products the net trading position is as might be expected: the Bloc is a net exporter of the simpler processed products, butter and cheese, and a net importer, although in relatively small quantities, of dried milk. Eggs are an increasingly important export. For vegetables the Bloc has retained its position as an exporter of potatoes and pulses, but in 1958 some imports of onions were necessary. The Bloc is an overall exporter of grapes and pears but finds it necessary to import apples. Live cattle must be imported; 50,000 head were bought in 1961. Live pigs however are generally exported although in 1961 this position was reversed and the Bloc imported 121,000 head.

Imports of tropical and semi-tropical produce have tended to remain stable, despite pressures on the Bloc from the tropical producers, and represent a very small proportion of the total world imports. Bloc imports of tea and coffee, less a small quantity of re-exports, amount to less than 2.5 per cent of the total world imports of each commodity. The Soviet market accounts for about 6 per cent of world imports of cocoa beans. Imports of fruit represented only 0.6 per cent of the world imports of bananas in 1961, of citrus fruit the Bloc total was 6 per cent, of dates almost 10 per cent, and of raisins and currants nearly 8 per cent. World trade in soya beans, however, is dominated by the Soviet Bloc which took 55.7 per cent of the total of world imports; the only major importing countries outside the Bloc are Japan, which accounted for 28.7 per cent of the world total in 1961, and West Germany, 22.5 per cent.

Thus despite its dependence on the export of food and food products as one of its main sources of foreign exchange the Soviet Bloc is not particularly well placed from the point of view of exportable surpluses. A comparison between the Soviet Bloc's average trade position over the four years 1958-61 and U.S. exports shows the great American preponderance in cereals, and the reverse in the case of prepared meat and eggs.

COMPARATIVE EXPORTS
'000 tons

	Total Bloc	U.S.S.R.[a]	U.S.
Wheat	703	4,801	19,929[a]
Rye	267	1,088	219[a]
Barley	482[a]	1,007	1,367[a]
Maize	412	406	7,447[a]
Oats	208	180	255[a]
Total grains	2,072	7,481	29,217[a]
Prepared and canned meat	77[a]	1	38
Eggs (no. million)	1,234	-	245

a. 1961 only. b. This is not a true guide but represents only an export potential if all grains were grown in surplus in the same year.

The table above presents the Soviet Bloc's export position in the most favourable light since the average for the left hand column is calculated only for the years when the Bloc had an exportable surplus. Thus it is clear that the Bloc as a whole had a larger exportable grain surplus than the U.S. only in the case of rye, although there was little difference in the volume of oats available for export. The U.S.S.R. itself, however, is a considerably larger exporter of rye than the U.S., and falls not far short in barley and oats. The major difference is that the U.S. would never be in the Soviet Bloc's position of requiring massive imports of wheat to compensate for shortfalls in domestic production, as happened in 1963. In eggs and processed meat the Bloc is well ahead of the U.S. as an exporter.

COUNTRY BY COUNTRY BALANCE

The Soviet Union itself is a net exporter of temperate grains (1.8 million tons in 1961), except in seasons of a crop failure; of butter, 47,000 tons in 1961; and generally of fresh meat, which in 1961 amounted to 13,000 tons net. The main exports of the Eastern European countries are as follows;

Bulgaria is a net exporter of fresh and processed meat; temperate fruit; vegetables; dairy products on a minor scale and eggs in considerable volume (in 1961 its exports of 534 million represented over 25 per cent of the whole Bloc's net exports in that year). It is also a major supplier of live pigs.

Czechoslovakia: sugar, which rose to 709,000 tons, net, in 1961, and eggs, 80,000 million net in 1961, are the main exports, while there is also a surplus of some fruit and vegetables, usually amounting to only a few thousand tons.

East Germany is a net exporter of one product only, sugar, of which net sales abroad were nearly 300,000 tons in 1961.

Hungary: the main exports are live cattle and pigs, of which 92,000 head of the former were sold in 1961 and a net total of 57,000 pigs; fresh meat exports are also large, amounting to 23,000 tons net in 1961. Of dairy products, net exports of butter in 1961 were 2,000 tons, of cheese 8,000 tons and of eggs 132 million. Sugar exports reached nearly 200,000 tons in 1961, and useful supplies of all types of fruit and vegetables were exported, almost entirely to other Bloc members.

Poland: meat and dairy produce have been developed as major export lines and a considerable business has been built up, as far as possible directed to Western markets. In 1961 fresh meat exports amounted to 74,000 tons, while those of canned and processed meat, the bulk of which consists of bacon and other other processed forms of pigmeat, were 85,000 tons; this was rather higher than the net exports of the Bloc of 77,000 tons. Poland is the leading egg exporter of the Bloc with sales of 1,443 million in 1961, or nearly 70 per cent of the Bloc's net exports, while butter exports were 27,000 tons and cheese, net, 3,000 tons. Other exports are fruit and vegetables, of which the most important single item is potatoes amounting to some 162,000 tons in 1961.

Rumania, together with the Soviet Union, is the granary of the Bloc; in 1961 net exports of grain amounted to 676,000 tons, or over half of the total grain surplus of the Bloc; the principal cereal is maize. In a year of poor crops, however, this export surplus can dwindle to little more than 50,000 tons, as in 1959. Another major export is sugar, while dairy produce, fresh meat, eggs, fruit and pulses are produced in exportable surpluses.

The picture of trade in the Soviet Bloc is completed by a brief examination of the pattern of food imports.

The Soviet Union imports large quantities of soya beans, 2.18 million tons in 1961, eggs (161 million), cattle (138,000 head) and pigs (209,000 head). Net imports of processed and canned meat in 1961 amounted to no more than 5,000 tons. Total imports ot temperate fruit probably totalled about 200,000 tons per annum. Prior to 1960 the U.S.S.R. imported 100-200,000 tons of sugar a year, but since Cuba became an economic responsibility of the Soviet Bloc the Soviet Union's net imports of sugar rose to over 2.6 million tons in 1961, and this despite an increase in exports from about 200,000 tons to almost 1 million. Rice imports also fall into a similar category of politically motivated trade; in 1960 imports amounted to 500,000 tons but in 1960 these had been cut back to the more economically justified total of 20,000 tons. Coffee imports totalled 30,000 tons in 1961 but although the U.S.S.R. was able to export 6,000 tons to other Bloc countries, it was still left with substantial net imports that are not in much demand in the Soviet Union, which is virtually exclusively a tea drinking country. Tea is imported according to need and a few thousand tons are re-exported to other Bloc countries. Considerable quantities of citrus and other tropical fruit are imported for domestic consumption.

Bulgaria fluctuates between being a net importer and a net exporter of grains; in 1960 it produced an export surplus of 19,000 tons but in 1961 this position was reversed and net imports were 20,000 tons. The sugar position is somewhat similar; in 1960 exports exceeded imports by 2,000 tons but in the following year net imports were 32,000 tons, probably because of the general surplus of Cuban sugar within the Bloc.

Czechoslovakia is a substantial net importer of grains; these totalled almost 1.5 million in 1961, of which 1.1 million tons was wheat. Imports of rice are large, amounting to 163,000 tons in 1961. Soya beans are a significant import. Net imports of fresh meat in 1961 were 80,000 tons plus a further 5,000 tons of canned or processed meat; 17,000 head of pigs and 7,000 of cattle were bought. Imports of butter amounted to 17,000 tons. 138,000 tons of potatoes were imported net in 1961, 12,000 tons of pulses and large quantities of tropical fruit and apples.

E. Germany: like West Germany it depends on imports to provide foodstuffs for a mainly industrial economy. Imports of grains in 1961 were over 1.9 million tons, the next largest after Poland. Fresh meat imports were 106,000 tons while 100,000 head of pigs were imported. Dairy produce imports are the largest in the Bloc with butter at 51,000 tons, cheese at 21,000 tons and eggs, 20 million. Imports of potatoes, net, in 1961 reached 89,000 tons while those of other vegetables, temperate and tropical fruit and tropical beverages were all substantial.

Hungary is a net importer of grains, with a total of 538,000 tons in 1961. Soya bean imports vary from over 60,000 tons to under 20,000. Small quantities of coffee and cocoa are imported and some 20,000 tons of citrus fruit.

Poland is the largest grain importer in the Bloc with a total of over 2.3 million tons in 1961, of which 1.74 million tons were wheat. 60,000 tons of rice were also bought while imports of soya beans fluctuate widely, from about 50,000 tons to under 25,000. Sugar imports shot up from 45,000 tons in 1959 to 261,000 in 1961, as a result of exchanges with Cuba. 36,000 tons of citrus fruit were imported in 1961 and 10,000 tons of cocoa.

Rumania is a net importer only of citrus fruit, 13,000 tons in 1961, and small quantities of cocoa and potatoes and other vegetables.

THE IMPORTANCE OF TRADE IN FOOD PRODUCTS

To assess the importance of foreign and inter-Bloc trade in food and food products, an examination of these exchanges in relation to overall trade must be made in value terms. With all trade in which the Soviet countries are involved it is extremely difficult to fix exact values on any transactions, partly because of the variable rates of exchange at which it is possible to convert Communist currencies to US$ and partly because of the unreliability of the value ratings given in the original Soviet sources. For these reasons the values shown below are no more than approximate.

THE VALUE OF TRADE IN FOOD AND FOOD PRODUCTS
US$ million

	1958	1959	1960	1961	1962
U.S.S.R.					
Imports					
Food and beverages[a]	609	606	656	780	742
Total	4,350	5,073	5,629	5,828	6,450
Exports					
Food and beverages	607	802	693	813	936
Total	4,298	5,440	5,560	5,998	7,035
Bulgaria					
Imports					
Food and beverages	25	29	32	26	44
Total	367	580	633	666	780
Exports					
Food and beverages	145	166	219	261	282
Total	373	467	572	662	770
Czechoslovakia					
Imports					
Food and beverages	340	383	400	374	384
Total	1,357	1,602	1,816	2,024	2,071
Exports					
Food and beverages	113	116	110	138	107
Total	1,513	1,785	1,994	2,120	2,187

THE VALUE OF TRADE IN FOOD PRODUCTS
US$ million

	1958	1959	1960	1961	1962
East Germany					
Imports					
Food and beverages	...	...	...	...	...
Total	1,680	1,992	2,170	2,216	2,371
Exports					
Food and beverages	...	...	...	...	...
Total	1,890	2,121	2,191	2,261	2,375
Hungary					
Imports					
Food and beverages	60	71	81	108	110
Total	631	793	976	1,025	1,148
Exports					
Food and beverages	162	174	179	203	217
Total	684	770	874	1,029	1,100
Poland					
Imports					
Food and beverages	195	240	239	257	251
Total	1,224	1,419	1,495	1,688	1,886
Exports					
Food and beverages	214	209	239	322	316
Total	1,060	1,146	1,326	1,505	1,647
Rumania					
Imports					
Food and beverages	...	...	...	...	...
Totals	482	502	648	815	941
Exports					
Food and beverages	...	...	...	...	...
Total	468	522	717	793	818

a. Including oilseeds. ... Not available.

Source FAO and national sources.

During the five-year period covered in the table above, the U.S.S.R. was a net exporter of foodstuffs in each year except 1958 when there was a small surplus of imports. As a result of the poor harvest of 1963 and the failure of the cereal crops in the virgin lands, it is virtually certain that an excess of imports over exports will again be recorded. Trade in food products is not generally to be relied on to earn a substantial surplus of foreign currency; only in 1959 and 1962 was the difference in value between exports and imports greater than $40 million. In these good years, however, the difference was almost $200 million, which is a significant contribution to Russia's import potential, geared, as this has always been in the past, to the barter principle by which trade must always be balanced in value, although preferably showing an export surplus.

In all years of good cereal crops the Soviet Union has attempted to export to non-Communist countries and to import food from within the Bloc, thus reserving its foreign exchange earnings of non-Bloc currencies for the purchase of Western capital goods. Imports of foodstuffs average about 12 per cent of the total value of imports, while food exports fluctuate from 12 to 15 per cent of the total. The movements of both imports and exports follow the variations in internal production. By way of comparison, U.S. exports of foodstuffs repre ented 17.6 per cent of total sales abroad by value in 1961 and were four times as large as Russian food exports in that year. Despite the much more highly industrialised economy of the U.S. this value was mostly accounted for by un-processed foodstuffs including however, frozen poultry which is the product of a sophisticated agricultural system.

Bulgaria is a substantial exporter of foodstuffs; this item forms between 36 and 39 per cent of all exports. Food usually accounts for about 5 per cent of the total import bill. In 1961 and 1962 the net earnings of trade in foodstuffs were over $230 million per year which is the highest margin in the Bloc, with the possible exception of Rumania for which no statistics are available. Like Bulgaria, Hungary is a net exporter of foodstuffs; it accounted for 22.6 per cent of the total in 1959 and 19.7 per cent in 1961 and 1962. Food purchases account for around 10 per cent of all imports and the net balance since 1960 has amounted to over $100 million a year. Rumania is also a very substantial net exporter of foodstuffs, mainly unprocessed. It is impossible to obtain the value of its trade but it is reasonable to assume that the export of food products represents about a quarter of total exports, giving a value in 1961 and 1962 of around $200 million. It is probable that imports were worth $20-30 million in the same years, or 2-4 per cent of total purchases.

Poland is also a net exporter of foodstuffs by value in normal years, but because this trade relies partly on the added value of processing imports and partly on livestock which must be fed on imported cereals it is susceptible to fluctuations due to climatic conditions. In the five years shown above Poland achieved a net gain of exports over import value in three separate years, a net deficit for one year and a balance in the one year remaining. In 1961 and 1962 the net earnings in this trade in food and food products were over $60 million a year. Over the whole period food exports have accounted for 18-22 per cent of the total, while imports fell from the 16-17 per cent of 1958 and 1959 to 13 per cent in 1961. On the whole Poland concentrates on selling its processed foodstuffs in the West to pay for imports of machinery and equipment.

Czechoslovakia maintains a very large imbalance in its trade in food products. In each year shown on the table on p. 34 Czechoslovakia has had to find well over $200 million, or goods to an equivalent value, to pay for its excess of imported foodstuffs over exports, mainly of processed food products. This very large food bill is the highest in the Bloc with the possible exception of East Germany's. The percentage of food to total imports is slowly falling from 25 per cent in 1958 to 18.5 per cent in 1962, but judging from the general apparent scarcity of food in Czechoslovakia it is possible that this downward trend may not be maintained consistently over the coming five years. Similarly exports of foodstuffs are graduallyf assuming less importance as a contribution to the total foreign trade earnings; in 1958 they represented 7.4 per cent, in 1960, 5.5 per cent, and in 1962, 4.9 per cent. No statistics are available for East Germany but it is probable that the overall pattern is not unlike that of Czechoslovakia. Imports of food possibly account for 20-23 per cent of the total import bill, or $410-450 million in 1962. Exports are probably worth only some $50 million a year or less, which would be about 2 per cent of total exports in 1962.

CHAPTER 4 MARKET OPERATIONS AND TRADE PROSPECTS

OVERALL POLICY CONSIDERATIONS

The policy of the Soviet Bloc in its interventions into the world foodstuff markets is based on political as well as economic motives. In operating its import policy the Bloc is handicapped by a number of political obligations. The best known of these is the commitment to Cuba to buy the bulk of its sugar crop to compensate for the loss of sales to the U.S., although Cuban sugar is an economic liability to the Bloc countries. In the same way fish which is not needed in the U.S.S.R. is purchased from Iceland for political reasons, as is coffee from Colombia and Brazil, cocoa from Ghana and rice from Burma. Since the purpose of these operations is to make a contribution to the economies of the supplying countries, the prices at which the Communist countries buy are usually equal to, if not above, the world market level. There are signs, however, that the Bloc is gradually modifying its willingness to buy surpluses from underdeveloped countries unless the political gains are considerable or unless a reasonably worthwhile level of reciprocal trade can be built up. This became evident in the relations of the newly independent East African states with the Soviet Union and other Bloc countries.

Both Tanganyika and Kenya hoped to find substantial outlets for their primary products in Eastern Europe but missions from the two countries each found the Communists disappointingly unenthusiastic. The government of Kenya was extremely anxious to sell a large proportion of its surplus coffee to the Soviet Bloc, but its ministers returned from Europe in December 1963 with an actual order for only 250 tons of coffee annually although vague promises had been made that the U.S.S.R. would take 10,000 tons a year in five years' time. In return Kenya agreed to import goods to equivalent value from the Eastern Bloc, which is a hard bargain for Kenya since it can buy more cheaply from India and Japan. It is significant that the mission from Kenya to Eastern Europe was the first attempt after Kenya became independent to establish new trade links: thus Moscow must have taken a political decision not to enter into a trade agreement with Kenya which would play a major role in supporting the economy of that country, if the price was to be large imports of unneeded coffee. In this case economic considerations seem to have outweighed political opportunities to make new friends.

Apart from purchases from underdeveloped countries which are intended as a form of economic aid in order to fulfil political objectives, the Bloc's other imports of food products are based on satisfying domestic requirements. Imports of grain from Western countries, such as the heavy purchases contracted for at the end of 1963 and in the early months of 1964, are taken up only because of the shortfall of domestic output. The Soviet Bloc is exceedingly reluctant to buy food from the West since this involves the loss of exchange which could be used on capital equipment badly needed as part of the economic development programmes of the Bloc countries. In fact, under the Stalin regime shortages of food in the Bloc did not usually affect the foreign trade policy. If there was not enough food it was accepted that the people must go hungry and, indeed, there were occasions when the Soviet government exported grain during a severe domestic food crisis either in order to purchase equipment or for purely political motives. Under Mr. Khrushchev, far more attention has been paid to raising living standards within the Bloc. This is slowly creating a situation in which certain demand factors can be said to be operating. Under Stalin consumer demand was a non-existent concept since the state decreed what should be supplied to the domestic consumers. Under the leadership of Mr. Khrushchev the Russian consumer has assumed much more importance in official policy. While it is still far from clear whether Mr. Khrushchev is seen to stress the interests of Soviet citizens because of political necessity to secure his position against other powerful factions in the Party, or because he is genuinely anxious to make a complete break with former practice and to usher in better living conditions as the next stage in the development of Communism in Russia and so show the non-Communist countries that the Soviet system can produce the same standards of living as obtain in the West, trade policy is now firmly aimed in the direction of meeting the food requirements of the population.

In these terms the Soviet Union's interventions in world markets in the future can be predicted more easily than when policy was motivated by political rather than economic reasons. In buying foodstuffs on the world market the U.S.S.R. will seek to meet its own domestic needs which in normal years are confined to tropical fruits, soya beans, some dried food and pulses, rice and tea. Other needs such as those for eggs, live cattle, fresh deciduous fruit and, prior to the realignment of Cuba, sugar are met as far as possible by imports from Bloc countries. With its political commitments the Soviet Union is unable to adhere strictly to this pattern. Because of its relations with Cuba the Soviet Union is obliged to import massive quantities of unwanted sugar; because of Bloc shortages or shortages in overseas countries which rely for support on the Eastern Bloc, of which the classic case is again Cuba, Russia is forced to export large quantities of grain which it would prefer to use for domestic consumption or for export to Western countries where such sales would earn hard currency. The Soviet Union is also at the mercy of the weather since a bad harvest can wipe away its export surpluses at almost a single stroke.

Thus if the U.S.S.R. is to pursue a policy of importing only against its domestic requirements and to abandon a politically orientated import policy it will need to establish a higher degree of self-sufficiency than exists at the moment. At present Soviet hopes of achieving self-sufficiency are bedevilled by the need to supply foodstuffs to other Bloc countries and outside dependencies. Its efforts to persuade the Eastern European countries to aim at self-sufficiency on their own, and to maintain an export surplus for Russian requirements, have not met with great success, partly because Rumania, which is the major producer of grains outside Russia in the Bloc, is not prepared to accept its role in the economic framework of the Bloc as a mere granary. In cases of shortages within the Bloc it would be unrealistic not to accept that the most economic method of making up requirements is from other Bloc suppliers but this is often an unpalatable truth to the Soviet officials responsible for foreign trade. From the point of view of each single Bloc country, trade planners are obliged to examine the situation in unilateral terms.

This arises from the Communist concept of trade as a series of bilateral exchanges each unrelated to trade with other countries except to the extent that hard currency earned by the Bloc need not be spent in the country in which it was earned. The basic principle upon which Soviet trade is based is that of exchanges between two partners which will balance exactly at the end of the year. Thus in all its trade agreements with the outside world the Soviet Union sets a level at which trade in both directions should aim. Although these arrangements are considered in money values they are essentially barter deals in which the value of the commodities traded in one direction is as nearly as possible equal to the value of the trade in the opposite direction. The original purpose of this attitude towards trade was to overcome the difficulties arising from the inconvertibility of the rouble; if the trade between the U.S.S.R. and one of its partners exactly balanced no problems need arise with its trading partners over holdings of roubles which could only be used in the Eastern Bloc and even then possibly at a disadvantageous exchange rate: a sufficient deterrent to scare off most Western countries for some years. Of course the aim of trade policy was, and remains, to ensure a surplus of exports to any given trading partner over imports, but in fact this situation is almost impossible to achieve with hard currency countries. Usually the U.S.S.R. is most anxious to import from the highly industrialised Western countries, but in return it has little to offer that is attractive to them as imports from the Soviet Union, other than raw materials or foodstuffs which are not always available in sufficient quantities for export. Again the Soviet Union is often anxious to export grains, for example, of which a surplus already exists in the world markets. Hence the Soviet Union is obliged to resort to the bilaterally balanced trade pattern since it is highly likely that if it traded freely on a multilateral payments basis it would rapidly run up a formidable trade deficit especially with the highly industrialised countries of the West.

This concept of trade has not only been applied to dealings with the non-Communist countries but also governs inter-Bloc trade. The situation seems to have its roots in the weaknesses of all Eastern currencies, and the impossibility of using gold or hard Western currencies as an inter-Bloc means of exchange. In practice it often involves straight barter deals such as the shipment of machinery to Hungary from East Germany against a return shipment of foodstuffs. Even basing trade on this relatively unsophisticated barter principle the Bloc has run into difficulties. How, for example, can relative values of a consignment of machine tools be assessed in terms of tons of potatoes and beef? Since there was a basic currency convertibility problem which prevented exchanges based on money transactions there was no common ground on which to calculate the value of imports against exports. Consequently inter-Bloc trade has been complicated by difficulties in assessing nominal prices, and on occasions Western market prices have been used, although this does not resolve the difficulties involved in comparing the 'value' of agricultural produce with that of manufactured goods, especially when the manufactured goods are specialised machine tools and of inferior quality to any equivalent that might be offered by Western manufacturers. Eventually an attempt was made by the Eastern Bloc to arrange a multilateral payments system for trade within Comecon; at the end of 1964 a clearing bank is to be established through which all trade transactions may be carried out. It will, however, be some years before the members of Comecon use its potential to the full as in the meantime they must abandon an entire philosophical attitude towards trade and replace it with a fully Westernised money concept. The Bloc has not yet come to grips with the problems of establishing a monetary system in which all members of the Bloc can have confidence, and this, too, will delay full utilisation of the multilateral payments facilities. Thus within the Bloc the present situation is likely to be maintained until economic needs compel a radical change in attitude by all member countries.

In the meantime food products will continue to be regarded as a kind of trading currency and the Soviet Union will attempt to reinforce its position in two main directions. Internally the Soviet Union is committed to an ambitious programme of expanding its food production. One leg of this scheme, which was the policy of developing the virgin lands (see p. 8), failed disastrously in 1963, and consequently Mr. Khrushchev has found it necessary to revise not only agricultural policy but a great range of industrial targets as well. In fact there is no reason why the U.S.S.R. should not raise its annual output of grains by 20-25 per cent, even when production in the virgin lands is discounted completely. The key to increased yields lies in the techniques used to encourage the labour force and the availability of chemical fertilisers; an effort has been made by the State to tackle both these problems. Results in agriculture tend to be slow but it is likely that by the end of the decade the U.S.S.R. will have achieved self-sufficiency in grains in all but the most exceptional years, and that even in seasons when severe crop failures occur the net shortfall will be much reduced. Thus the possible need for the Soviet Union to intervene in the world grain market on the scale of its operations in 1963 should disappear by 1970. Nevertheless there could be a similar year of bad harvests before that date and an examination of the sequence of events in 1963 will indicate the Soviet method of entering the market as a major purchaser.

WHEAT AND BREAD GRAINS

The 1963 crop failure and its effects

In normal years the Soviet Union can rely on its domestic wheat production to serve a number of purposes; supply to the Russian population, export to other Bloc countries, and a surplus for export outside the Bloc. In part this situation came about because of Mr. Khrushchev's initiative in launching a campaign for the reclamation of the virgin lands in the north of Kazakhstan and the south of Siberia. The work first got under way in the 1954-5 season. In the years since the Revolution this area had been devoted to pasture, but now efforts were made, at heavy capital cost, to turn the area into a grain belt. In 1958 a bumper harvest in these virgin lands of 14 million tons contributed to a total grain output of 141 million tons, of which 76.6 million tons were wheat. This enabled exports to be maintained at near the very high 1957 level of 7.3 million tons, of which 5.45 million tons were wheat. Compared with the 1955 performance of 3.7 million tons of all grains available for export, and 1956 showed an even lower total - 3.2 million tons of which 1.5 million tons were wheat - the level maintained from 1957 onwards was a major breakthrough. In 1962 wheat exports were 4.76 million tons out of a total of 7.8 million tons. Of the total wheat exported, however, some 70 per cent on average was bought by Communist countries including, after 1960, Cuba. In 1962 this was distributed as shown in the table below.

SOVIET EXPORTS OF WHEAT TO OTHER COMMUNIST COUNTRIES IN 1962

	'000 tons	Percentage of all exports
Eastern Europe		
E. Germany	1,251	26.3
Czechoslovakia	903	18.9
Poland	505	10.6
Bulgaria	94	2.0
Hungary	40	0.9
Total	2,793	58.7
China	104	2.2
Cuba	269	5.6
Grand Total	3,166	66.5

In addition to the supplies to Communist countries the U.S.S.R. has commitments under bilateral trade agreements to supply wheat to Finland and Brazil. In 1962 Brazil bought 412,800 tons and Finland 219,400 tons. Thus after meeting these demands there was only a relatively small margin of Soviet wheat left over for sale to the U.K., Netherlands or West Germany, its best customers and the countries from which imports would be of the utmost value to the Soviet economy.

In 1963 the harvest failed to produce the normal yields in the traditional cereal lands and at the same time the crop from the virgin lands fell to a mere 5 million tons which was probably not even enough to support the workers who have either been moved into the area or who are indigenous to it. Total wheat output was probably rather less than 50 million tons. Because of the heavy demands that are made on Soviet grain production it is almost certain that the 1963 production shortfall was considerably aggravated by the dearth of stocks. Exports of the order aimed at in Soviet policy during a period when more food is being made available for an expanding urban population, and when livestock numbers are increasing and thus requiring larger quantities of fodder, can have left little scope or opportunity in recent years for building up Soviet stocks. In fact, the trend must almost certainly have been the reverse and stocks ran down to very small reserves.

Hence for a combination of reasons the Soviet Union and the Comecon countries were faced with a serious grain shortage when the 1963 harvest had been gathered.

The first reactions may have been due to an over-pessimistic assessment of the situation. In September the Soviet Union informed Finland that it must stop its deliveries of wheat which were still due under the terms of the Finno-Soviet trade agreement for 1963; of the total quota of 270,000 tons the shortfall amounted to 60,000 tons. When the 1964 trade agreement was negotiated the Soviet delegation was extremely reluctant to include wheat among the Russian exports. Although Finland is virtually self-sufficient in cereals it insisted that wheat be included because of the difficulty in finding a suitably saleable alternative import from the U.S.S.R., and Russia, under pressure, agreed to set the quota at 130,000 tons. In October Russia defaulted on grain deliveries to Norway and as a result only 55,000 tons of the 120,000 tons quota for 1963 was fulfilled. By the end of 1963 the trade agreement with Brazil had virtually lapsed because of the inability of the U.S.S.R. to export grain.

The response to the crisis was not confined to exports to its non-Communist trading partners. Already in 1962 the U.S.S.R. had limited its deliveries of wheat to Poland to only 505,000 tons instead of the 600,000 tons agreed in the trade agreement between the two countries. This tends to support the view that Russia had been suffering from heavy pressure on its stocks before the bad harvest of 1963. In the 1964 agreement trade in food products is to be restricted to those foods which are in surplus in either country; in the case of exports from the Soviet Union this covers only tea. This indicates that Russia is unable to commit itself to supplying other Bloc countries and that they must buy on the world market.

At the same time the Soviet Union was making its own incursions on the world market. In August 1963, when it was clear that the Soviet harvest would not be a good one, it contracted for 11 million bushels of wheat from Canada, its first purchase in that market since February 1961 and its largest contract since the 1957-8 crop year. In September further contracts were placed in Canada amounting to some 6.8 million tons and including 16.5 million bushels of wheat for delivery to Cuba. Thus at this point the Soviet Union was obliged to buy on the world market to fulfil its own commitments to a Communist trading partner. In September Russia con tracted to buy 300,000 tons of wheat flour from West Germany; it was estimated that this was based on one part in four of U.S. wheat. On this occasion the Russian entry into the world market was marked by great political soul-earching in W. Germany before export licences were issued. By the end of the year the Soviet Union had negotiated wheat deals with Australia and France as well as making an approach to U.S. grain shippers.

At the same time the Soviet grain shortage had been felt with varying intensity by its Comecon partners. In March 1963 Czechoslovakia contracted for 120,000 tons of Canadian wheat; in July and August Poland undertook to purchase 7.4 million bushels but by November its contract for Canadian wheat totalled 29.4 million bushels, while Czechoslovakia had ordered 1.2 million tons. In October 1963 Bulgaria bought 300,000 tons of Canadian wheat, while East Germany and Hungary shopped in the U.S. market.

The significance of these purchases is greater in respect to the U.S.S.R. than to the Eastern European countries, which are fairly regular buyers of grains from Western suppliers. The Soviet Union is also an irregular purchaser on the world market at times of shortages, but the 1963-4 season's contracts were on an unprecedentedly large scale and for the first time Russia turned to the U.S. as a source of grain. Furthermore there was no question that these imports could be paid for out of the earnings of Soviet exports, or from reserves of foreign currency accruing from trading surpluses; instead it was freely admitted, even in the U.S.S.R., that gold was used to finance the transactions. By the nature of the deliveries, some of which extend to April 1966, it is probable that the Soviet Union has accepted that it will be dependent, in the short-term at least, on supplies of grain from the West.

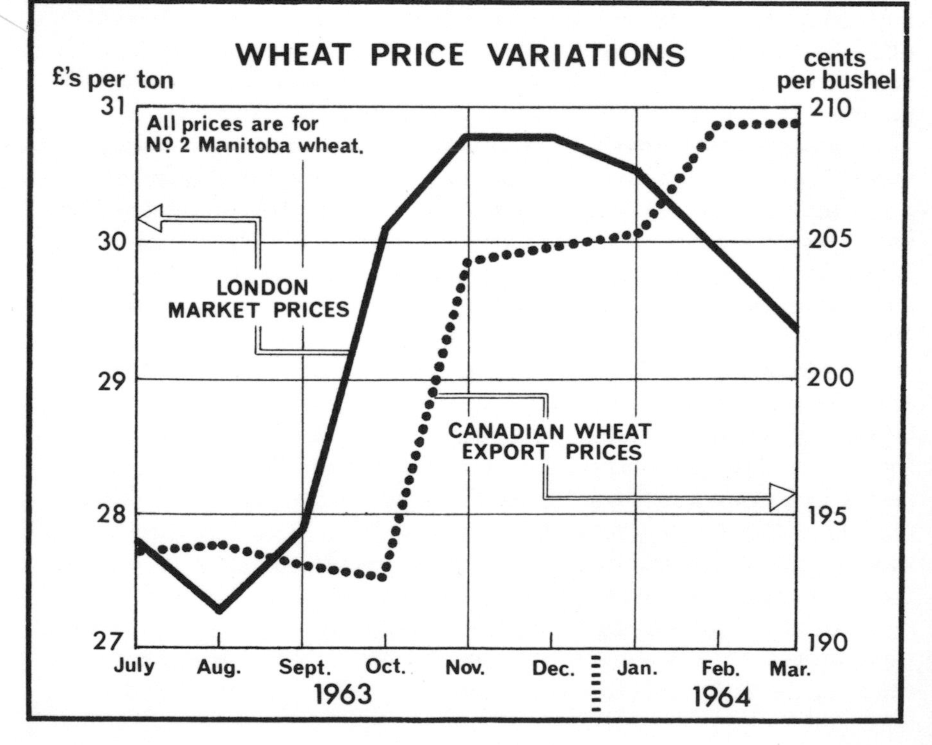

The effects of the Soviet purchases on the suppliers and on the wheat market were to bring about an unexpected rally in prices in a period of relative depression. The Canadian growers, who benefited most from the orders placed, were relieved of heavy stocks, some of which they had almost given up all hopes of selling, and not only obtained better prices for their 1963 crop but were assured of being able to sell it. In addition there is secured demand for the forward supplies for which the Soviet Union has contracted. At a time of generally low morale the Russian purchases put new heart into the Canadian wheat market.

The effect on prices is shown in the chart on p.44. The London market was not directly involved and thus the price movements reflect the general effects on the world market. The Canadian export price, however, moved in line with supplies and hence as Soviet purchases mounted so the stocks of wheat available for export fell. Thus Canadian export prices continued high as a result of Soviet purchases and the shipments of orders whereas the London market dropped back after the U.S.S.R. and Eastern European countries had completed their round of buying.

In the U.S. the Soviet orders failed to reach the levels that had first been predicted. It seems certain that in the early autumn of 1963 the Soviet authorities over-estimated their import requirements, either in terms of the gold available for release to pay for grain, or because on the final count the harvest was not quite as bad as had been first feared. At that time the U.S. government discussed sales to the U.S.S.R. of the order of 200 million bushels; in fact the whole Eastern Bloc bought less than 80 million bushels. Wheat orders of the magnitude of 200 million bushels would have raised U.S. exports of this commodity by about 25 per cent, which in the present state of wheat production would have represented a bumper year for U.S. growers and shippers. In fact the actual Soviet orders probably raised exports by 10 per cent for the 1963-4 season. Furthermore these purchases suggest that the U.S. will be on Russia's shopping list if it is again obliged to enter the world market for large scale purchases.

Future prospects for wheat

Even if the 1963 production crisis is not repeated the outlook for wheat in the short term is uncertain. Although the U.S.S.R. has decided on firm corrective action to avoid the bad management and mistakes of the past, it will take two or three seasons to restore wheat production to a level at which, given reasonable weather conditions, the Bloc will be able to dispense with imports. This is a matter of shifting back to growing wheat in areas where previously maize had been planted at the insistence of the planners and has failed to produce a yield in any way comparable with that normally achieved by wheat in the same area (see also p. 8). But the balance between self-sufficiency and shortfall in the wheat crop will be at the mercy of the weather.

In the long term, probably by the early 1970's, permanent import substitution will be achieved. With Russia's vast agricultural potential which has still to be exploited efficiently, there should be little difficulty in producing an assured surplus of 6 million tons a year for export. In view of the present state of supply of wheat this can only serve to swell a world surplus of wheat. This situation might well embarass the Soviet government as much as it would alarm Western wheat growers. On the basis of the present methods of intervention in world food markets such a surplus could mean that the U.S.S.R. will revert to selling cereals at low prices, as it has done in the past with the sole aim of acquiring enough foreign exchange to finance imports of goods it requires for its programme of industrial expansion.

This underlines the fundamental weakness of the barter concept of foreign trade. A trade agreement negotiated with a Western country is aimed at providing the U.S.S.R. with capital goods and other manufactures which it badly needs, and admits to needing. While Western countries are generally anxious to sell, since the capital goods industry can rarely afford to ignore an order, least of all Russian orders which are generally large, there is little that they need or that will appeal to the sophisticated Western consumer markets that the U.S.S.R. has to offer; hence the West will buy what is least unattractive or can be a substitute for imports from other countries. Wheat and other foodstuffs fall into this latter category. Because the Eastern Bloc can offer only a limited range of exports to a country from which it has committed itself to a list of purchases, it is in a very poor position to bargain over the price at which it will sell its wheat; by its nature this type of trade precludes offers on the world market. Thus the Soviet Union has not yet reached a point where it is able to command a price for grain, except where it is particularly dominant, as in inter-Bloc trade; nor has it attempted to sell on world market terms.

If U.S.S.R. production is increased to allow for a constant export surplus the world market price will tend to weaken, as a result of the disappearence of the Communist Bloc as purchasers, as well as because of the additional surplus available. This situation will make the world market less attractive to the U.S.S.R. and probably convince trade officials that they must maintain a bilateral system of trade by which wheat is offered at prices below the world market level. In turn this will serve to undermine the Western wheat suppliers, of which the North American growers would be the worst hit.

Alternatively there is the possibility that the Communist Bloc might come to recognise that the international market structure is a valuable one which it can put to profitable use. It is expected that the Soviet Bloc will slowly acquire a more sophisticated view of international marketing systems, and the move to base trade within Comecon on a multilateral payments system (see p. 40) indicates a tendency to accept the practical value of capitalist methods. Once the Soviet Union is faced with the problem of selling quantities of wheat on a regular basis trade officials must almost certainly examine what opportunities the international cereal markets offer, even if the actual system used is one of bilateral trade agreements. It would not require a great deal of knowledge of the wheat market to reveal to the Soviet government that a Russian wheat surplus could be used as a weapon in a deliberate attempt to upset the international wheat price structure. On the other hand it would also become clear that apart from causing confusion among Western producers, the U.S.S.R. would gain little beyond one season's advantage, and at the cost of rock-bottom prices which would come to be expected by the market as the normal Soviet level of wheat prices. Thus it is inevitable that when Russia becomes accustomed to being an annual wheat exporter the government will know that it possesses the power to undermine and disrupt the international wheat market. It is not likely, however, that the U.S.S.R. will adopt a policy of economic warfare in international food markets, partly because there would be little to gain in terms of export earnings, and possibly even a significant loss, and partly because there is scant evidence to suggest that the Communist Bloc has any real desire to assault the West in this way. Instead, it is probable that the U.S.S.R. will realise that barter-type trade is not the most satisfactory way to market exportable surpluses, and turn to the world market in an effort to obtain better prices. Since the advent of an export surplus of Russian wheat must weaken the market price, all producers will be concerned to restore price stability. If, at this point, the Soviet Union appreciates the fact that market stability depends on joint action between producing and consuming countries a co-operative attitude could well lead to an overall agreement on wheat which would benefit all producers. Thus if the U.S.S.R. decides to use the world wheat market it can only do so in agreement with other wheat producing countries, if the market is to return to a reasonably steady price level. This would mean that East-West co-operation in a world-wide commodity agreement for wheat would be necessary to maintain a usable mechanism.

OTHER COMMODITIES

Meat and Livestock

The Soviet Union and the countries of Eastern Europe buy beef and veal on the world market but not in very substantial quantities. The U.S.S.R. is the world's largest importer of sheep but these are supplied mainly by Mongolia and China; Mongolia also exports a large number of cattle to Russia. The Bloc buys from the West only in cases of specialised needs, e.g. the purchase of 100 Shorthorn cattle from Britain in October 1962 for breeding purposes at a cost of $61,600. The Bloc, however, is a major exporter of pigs and Poland is the largest exporting country in Europe, and second only to China. West Germany is Europe's largest market for live pigs and Poland is a steady supplier. Poland also is the world's second largest exporter of bacon and, since 1961, of pork. In addition it is the leading supplier of canned meat to West Germany. Its position in the British bacon market, together with that of the only other Communist exporting country, Hungary, is shown in the table below.

U.K. BACON IMPORTS

'000 tons	1958	1959	1960	1961	1962
Poland	48.7	49.3	47.9	48.5	50.9
Hungary	1.7	1.9	2.1	2.1	2.0
Total imports	343.5	353.1	411.9	400.7	404.9
Comecon percentage	14.6	14.5	12.1	12.6	13.1

The trade of Poland and Hungary with Britain remains almost stable in volume terms because exports are determined in the annual trade agreements drawn up with the U.K. Until 1962 Polish bacon was sold on the London Provision Exchange at prices below those obtained by equivalent grades of Danish, Dutch and British bacon, but in February of that year top grades of Polish bacon fetched slightly higher prices than Dutch, the next cheapest bacon from a major exporter, and remained ahead or on a par with Dutch for over six months.

The Eastern Bloc's livestock position is susceptible to marked variations from year to year and there seems little prospect of self-sufficiency being achieved in the short term. The increase in domestic consumption will also tend to absorb any permanent gains in output partly because of the steady expansion of population and also because of the trend towards higher living standards. Thus apart from Polish bacon exports there is unlikely to be any significant change in the Bloc's position in relation to selling on world markets in the next five years.

On the other hand there is the strong possibility of change in importing meat over the next five years. Although at present the Soviet government does not accept the need to maintain meat supplies at the same level each year, it cannot be long before meat and other high protein foods become regarded as essential and are granted priorities in the same way as wheat is a priority import when domestic production fails to satisfy minimum requirements. Soviet meat production falls considerably short of consumption; the gap is made up by imports, and because animal production in Russia is extremely inefficient it is certain to be a number of years before self-sufficiency can be achieved. The scope of the task that must be faced is indicated by some of the comments in Mr. Khrushchev's memorandum on agriculture sent to the Communist Party Central Committee in February 1964. The shortage of meat was emphasised by the injunction to double livestock production in Russia by using new techniques including the adoption of large-scale Western techniques which it necessary would be reinforced by importing plant, in the form of farm factories for pig breeding. While U.S. pig producers breed pigs by using 3-5 lbs of feedstuff per lb of pork, in Russia the ratio is 10-12 lbs of feedstuff to 1. Thus the reorganisation of techniques, which extends also to cattle and poultry, faces formidable problems. But since it is now accepted that meat production must be increased by almost any means available, it is but a short step to tacit recognition that meat plays a vital role in consumption, in fact to admitting that there is a demand for meat. Since this is likely to occur before domestic production can meet this demand the Soviet Bloc can be expected to become a larger purchaser of meat in world markets. In the long run it aims at self-sufficiency but it is probable that this cannot be achieved before 1975 at the earliest.

Sugar

Between 1950 and 1960 the Soviet Bloc was a net exporter of sugar, in most years of quantities of over 500,000 tons. Inside the Bloc the Soviet Union and Rumania were regular net importers. In 1960, however, the Castro revolution in Cuba and the subsequent alignment of Cuba with the Communist countries resulted in the import of 1.47 million tons of raw sugar by Russia and of some 200,000 tons by the Eastern European countries, thus swinging the balance of trade to an overall preponderance of imports over exports. In 1961 total Bloc imports amounted to 3.8 million tons while China and Albania imported a further 900,000 tons from Cuba. At the same time Eastern European countries exported over 2 million tons of sugar, mainly refined from the record domestic sugar beet crop of the 1960-61 season.

In 1961 imports by all Communist countries from Cuba represented 77 per cent of Cuba's total exports. Thus at one stroke Cuba effectively altered its role in the world sugar market. Prior to the crisis Cuba had acted as a buffer stock. After it had exported its International Sugar Agreement quota, which averaged 2.4 million tons a year, and had shipped its quota to the U.S. of around 2.9 million tons, Cuba generally still held stocks of 2-2.5 million tons. Because of the preferential prices paid by the U.S. for its quota purchases and U.S. financial backing, Cuba was able to serve as an extremely effective reserve supplier without suffering marked fluctuations in earnings. Once Cuba exported the bulk of its crop to the Soviet bloc, at prices below the U.S. preferential level, it became less worthwhile to act as a buffer stock. Also, in 1961-2 Cuban production fell from 6.8 million to 4.8 million tons, so wiping out its usual surplus after fulfilling quotas. The removal of Cuba's quotas from the U.S., and International Sugar Agreement markets, together with the loss of its stocks resulted in a gross reduction in supply of some 6 million tons of sugar on the world market, which was not compensated for by an equivalent increase in Soviet Bloc exports. In fact the 1962-3 sugar crisis arose because of a shortfall of roughly 3 million tons. This was clearly equivalent to the shortfall in Cuban production of 3.5 million tons. If Cuba had still been supplying the U.S. and International Sugar Agreement markets the crisis would have been scarcely perceptible since the absorption of the whole Cuban crop, which would have been the normal pattern, by Western markets would have virtually restored the balance.

The ensuing upheaval in sugar markets cannot be ascribed entirely to Soviet intervention in guaranteeing an outlet for the bulk of the Cuban crop. The price boom was caused by mismanagement and misjudgement as much as by the shortage of supplies, and this shortfall itself was a result of Cuba's own policy arising from the poor prices it earned for its sales on the non-Communist market in the previous year. Clearly the situation would not have taken place without Cuban realignment, but the crisis was a by-product rather than a direct and inevitable consequence.

Because of the alignment with the Soviet Bloc of the world's most important sugar supplier Moscow now has the potential power to manipulate the world market. In 1959 per caput sugar consumption in the Eastern Bloc was almost as high as in the European Economic Community but Russia could absorb considerable additional imports despite the fact that a large increase in domestic output is planned over the period 1960-70. China, however, is the really expansionary market since consumption was estimated as no more than 3 kg per head in 1958. Thus the whole Sino-Soviet area may be able to consume an additional 4-5 million tons of sugar imported annually from Cuba. Whether imports are absorbed or re-exported as refined sugar is almost entirely a question of policy. If the Soviet bloc reduces its net import total, or achieves a balance, the world market would be faced with virtually the same supply position as existed prior to the Cuban crisis, except that the world buffer stock would no longer be manageable as were the Cuban stocks. If a total of some 3 million tons of sugar is offered on the world market a situation of oversupply would be created and prices would drop. Alternatively, if the Communist Bloc remains a net importer for a few years only, world production will increase over this period, and with the offer of substantial exports from the Soviet countries a very large world surplus could be created, which would lead to difficulties for almost all producers.

In fact, however, it appears that the Soviet Union views the sugar situation with some caution. It uses Cuban sugar for inter-Bloc trade, e.g. in 1961 some 0·5 million tons of sugar were exported to China, and it has encouraged Cuba to cut back production. In 1962 the reduced Cuban production was not enough to meet its commitments to supply the Eastern Bloc, which were readily cut by half a million tons; even this lower quantity was too large for Cuba to supply. At the same time the Soviet Union has used sugar to make up some of its contracted exports under bilateral trade agreements with underdeveloped countries. Since Russia started importing from Cuba it has exported to Burma, Cambodia, Ceylon, Cyprus, Ethiopia, Ghana, Guinea, Iraq, Lebanon, Libya, Malaya, Mali, Morocco, Saudi Arabia, Somalia, Sudan, Togo and Zanzibar. Thus overall it is probable that Russia will seek to use its increased sugar supplies partly internally and partly for virtual barter with countries which are not otherwise significant sugar importers.

One of the side-effects of the Cuban crisis is that there is now a form of demand for sugar in the U.S.S.R. at a level which did not exist before 1961 (see p. 20), hence there is a limit on how much Cuban sugar will be free for re-export. The trade agreement drawn up in 1964 between Cuba and the Soviet Union makes provision for purchases of unrefined sugar of 2.1 million tons in 1965; 3 million tons in 1966; 4 million tons in 1967; and 5 million tons per annum over the next three years. The price has been set at the rate of 6 cents (U.S.) per lb for the whole period 1965-70 but payment will actually be made in goods. It is claimed by the Soviet Union that fixed prices iron out the fluctuations which affect open market prices. In fact, however, a barter agreement of this sort gives the Soviet Union a reasonable measure of freedom in which to make its own adjustments in the actual value of the goods exported since much of the pricing of these exports will be notional. It may well be that the working out of the Cuba-U.S.S.R. trade agreement will produce the same disagreements and mistrust which has arisen over similar arrangements within the Bloc under which food was bartered against machinery.

It is, however, now too late for Cuba to hope to rebuild its markets in the West. The international sugar market is restoring the loss in supply created by the Cuban revolution, and it would find it difficult to absorb 5-6 million tons of Cuban sugar if it again became available.

BEVERAGES - COFFEE, COCOA AND TEA

Coffee

The U.S.S.R. is a tea drinking country in which coffee consumption is negligible; in 1934-38 consumption was nil, but in 1903-13 consumption amounted to 0.07 kg per head. In 1961 it appeared to amount to 0.1 kg per head, but this may be far from accurate in practice. In Eastern Europe in 1961, consumption rose to its highest point since the war - 0.5 kg, compared with 0.8-0.9 kg - in the years prior to 1939. Purchases are mainly from Brazil, and cannot be seen as a deliberate policy to buy coffee as much as the outcome of a trade agreement signed because of the political importance of expanding Soviet influence in Latin America, as is the case with Russia's agreement with Colombia which also includes coffee. The unwillingness of the Bloc to buy coffee, which is doubtless regarded as an unnecessary luxury, is underlined in the negotiations with East African countries (see p. 37), when the Bloc undertook to import far less coffee than the Kenyans and Tanganyikans wanted to sell.

Nevertheless it is assumed that Soviet Bloc trade with coffee producing countries will increase and, as the standards of living rise in Eastern Europe, that coffee imports will be expanded to raise per caput consumption to nearer the level of Western Europe. But even if imports more than triple from 73,000 tons in 1961 to 250,000 tons in 1970, consumption per head in Eastern Europe would still be well below that in Western Europe. At present the scarcity of coffee in the Bloc enables the government to charge astronomic prices, which sometimes are the also inflated by inter-Bloc re-exporting, usually from the Soviet Union to Poland, Czechoslovakia or East Germany. But the overall criteria will be the availability of foreign exchange allied to possible political advantages to be derived from a trade agreement with a coffee-producing country. On the whole it is that latter factor which will be the most important in the next few years. Possibly by 1970 the government will respond to the latent demand for coffee by maintaining imports at no less than 250,000 tons a year. At this point the Soviet Bloc will be a normal coffee consumer with a need for regular supplies. At this stage it is probable that the Bloc will place more importance on the world market than on bilateral trade agreements with coffee-producing countries, since it may be politically more desirable to become a quota market, and thus appear to hold a responsible attitude towards the problems of developing countries, than to rely on a few producers, of which at least one Brazil, cannot be regarded as a stable trading partner.

Cocoa

As in the case of coffee, cocoa is one of the main agricultural products which cannot be grown within the Soviet Bloc and for which there are no suitable substitutes. Imports are regulated at present by a series of trade agreements; the U.S.S.R.-Ghana pact provides for a gradual increase in imports to reach 60,000 tons in 1965-6, and Russia has an agreement with Brazil, as have Poland and Bulgaria, which includes cocoa, and one with the Cameroun Republic. Gross imports in 1960 and 1961 averaged 82,000 tons, which represents about 8 per cent of world trade.

Consumption per head of cocoa beans was 0.15 kg in the Soviet Union in 1960 and 1961, and 0.45 kg in the Eastern European countries, compared with 0.05 kg per head pre-1939 in Russia and 0.5 kg in the other Bloc countries, which, in fact, is not very greatly out of line with consumption in other tea drinking countries, in the case of Russia, or, for Eastern European countries, a coffee-drinking nation such as Italy where cocoa consumption is about 0.6 kg per head. Thus the scope for expansion in relation to demand is not as great as in the case of coffee, but in fact imports will grow only as a result of decisions by the authorities in the short term. These will be governed by the same factors as influence coffee purchases, which are related not to consumption but to conditions of supply being particularly favourable to the Bloc economically or to political conditions being such as to make cocoa purchases from certain producers highly desirable. Because there is no great suppressed demand there will not be the same pressures on the Bloc, over the longer term, as with coffee, which might lead the Communist countries to use the international markets instead of trade agreements, although this could be the consequence of a general change of attitude.

Tea

The Soviet Union is the leading tea-drinking country in the Bloc and is also a producer. Russian consumption amounted to 0.26 kg per head in 1961 compared with an average of only 0.07 kg for the other Comecon members. Imports are not very large in world terms and the main supplier of the Soviet Union is generally China. India is the Bloc's main non-Communist source of tea but its imports in 1959 to 1961 of around 11,000 tons a year were less than 5 per cent of India's total exports of tea. At the same time Russia exports tea, the bulk going to Mongolia. By 1970 Russia plans to be self-sufficient in tea which will release China's exports of tea to the U.S.S.R. for sale on the world market and reduce the overall world import demand. The Eastern Bloc itself is unlikely to become a sizeable net exporter, but by increasing China's exportable surplus it will contribute to an important threat to equilibrium in the world market for tea.

CITRUS FRUIT

Consumption of citrus fruit in the Soviet Union and the Bloc countries of 0.6 kg per head in 1961 in the former and of 1.6 kg in Eastern Europe is very low compared with that in Western Europe; in France and Germany per caput consumption is 14-15 kg per year. The Eastern Bloc has ample opportunity to increase imports under its existing bilateral trade agreements with Morocco, Tunisia, Turkey, the United Arab Republic or Brazil, but has clearly chosen not to import large quantities of a commodity which can be regarded as a luxury, possibly because it would overstretch its potential supply of exportable commodities and manufactures to balance increased imports.

Over the rest of the sixties, however, the Bloc can be expected to raise its imports substantially. Poland, for example, plans to double its 1958 imports of citrus, of 35,000 tons by 1965, while East Germany plans to import some 150,000 tons by the same date, compared with about a third of this imported in 1961. Allowing for an overall increase in consumption without any great expansion of Soviet production, because of the high costs involved, total Bloc imports could amount to over 800,000 tons in 1970, some of which would be supplied by China. Doubtless purchases from non-Communist countries will be almost exclusively from producers with which Bloc countries have bilateral agreements, but increased purchases will help to relieve the situation of world surplus of citrus fruit.

A MOVE AWAY FROM BARTER

There are two radically opposed trends in Soviet trade with the outside world; one is represented by the initiative which has been taken in Comecon to set up a multilateral clearing bank so that inter-bloc trade can be conducted on the basis of freely convertible currency;

the other is represented by bilateral trade agreements and the principle that exchanges between the parties to the arrangement should balance, or, if possible, be in favour of the Communist country. There is also a somewhat similarly ambivalent attitude within Comecon on specialisation. The Soviet Union has been a firm upholder of economic specialisation within Comecon for some years and at last there are signs that in the field of trade with the West some specialisation is taking place. As the result of an unofficial, and unpublished, agreement between Comecon members it appears that Poland has been entrusted with making the Bloc's main purchases of grains and certain seeds; Czechoslovakia is responsible for buying industrial oilseeds; and East Germany purchases canned foods. This is borne out by large Polish wheat purchases made in late 1963 which were clearly intended to be re-exported to other Bloc countries, while Bulgarian imports of tobacco from the U.S. are known to have been shipped to the Soviet Union. This specialisation in foreign trading indicates that the Eastern Bloc is moving away from the concept of barter, or bilateral trade agreements since block purchases for re-export are too sophisticated to be handled by a series of bilateral arrangements both inside the Bloc and with outside suppliers.

On the other hand the specialisation of production, including growing foodstuffs, is based on a concept of trade by which one country produces enough wheat, for example, to exchange with its other Bloc partners for meat from one, machine tools from a second, dairy products from a third and tractors from a fourth. In a way this system depends on a bilateral trade principle. It is significant, however, that not all Comecon countries are as enthusiastic about specialisation of production as is the Soviet Union. In the case of Rumania it is clear that the government does not agree with the Soviet Union's views that its role should be confined to that of an agricultural producer without a heavy industry of its own. Thus nationalism is conflicting with the general plan for economic co-ordination.

As in the West change does not come easily in the Soviet Bloc. While there is a move forward in one sector there is a step backwards in another. But on the whole the pressures are for a switch of trade from the bilateral agreement basis to a multilateral payments system. It will take several years for a general change to take place since payment for foodstuffs in hard currencies, or gold, as in the case of the 1963-4 wheat purchases, are associated with extraordinary shortages. But by the time wheat surpluses are regularly produced for export it is likely that the Communist countries will have established a firmer base for their own currencies which may then be more widely used in international trade and will have found that the flexibility of a multilateral payments system has advantages over the rigidity of bilateral agreements. The latter, however, will doubtless be used for many years with underdeveloped countries and may even be used with developed countries to cover a certain minimum level of exchanges.

The next few years may be the last on the old pattern of Soviet Bloc needs, especially in grains. The new Soviet drive to improve yields, abandon misdirected policies, produce sufficient chemical fertilisers and mechanical aids, and to modernise livestock farming methods is the most important factor influencing the future relations of the Bloc with international markets for temperate foods. Once the Communist Bloc achieves a stable role in the temperate food markets it may come to play a larger role as a purchaser of tropical produce.

STATISTICAL APPENDIX

APPENDIX I: FOOD PRODUCTION

'000 tons

CEREALS

	1958	1959	1960	1961	1962
Wheat					
Bulgaria	2,334	2,427	2,379	2,034	2,060
Czechoslovakia	1,346	1,650	1,503	1,666	1,730[p]
E. Germany	1,363	1,371	1,456	1,038	...
Hungary	1,487	1,910	1,768	1,940	1,960
Poland	2,321	2,484	2,303	2,792	...
Rumania	2,914	4,000	3,450	3,990	...
Total	11,765	13,842	12,859	13,460	...
USSR	46,600	69,101	64,299	66,478	70,600
Total	58,365	82,943	77,048	79,938	...
Barley					
Bulgaria	444	560	622	612	...
Czechoslovakia	1,199	1,467	1,745	1,581	1,650[p]
E. Germany	931	1,039	1,269	947	...
Hungary	735	1,093	986	984	1,140
Poland	1,210	1,043	1,310	1,339	...
Rumania	305	449	405	468	...
Total	4,824	5,651	6,337	5,931	...
USSR	12,957	10,150	16,020	13,300	...
Total	17,781	15,801	22,357	19,231	...
Rye					
Bulgaria	102	97	82	70	50
Czechoslovakia	937	967	895	994	1,040[p]
E. Germany	2,368	2,133	2,126	1,504	...
Hungary	371	443	354	297	230
Poland	7,329	8,113	7,878	8,356	...
Rumania	124	128	103	104	...
Total	11,231	11,881	11,438	11,325	...
USSR	15,740	16,900	16,324	16,700	...
Total	26,971	28,781	27,762	28,025	...

APPENDIX I: (Continued)
'000 tons

CEREALS: (Continued)

	1958	1959	1960	1961
Oats				
Bulgaria	134	244	218	207
Czechoslovakia	871	929	1,020	959
E. Germany	1,143	966	1,007	856
Hungary	192	256	204	139
Poland	2,670	2,483	2,774	2,940
Rumania	250	315	284	275
Total	5,260	5,193	5,507	5,366
U.S.S.R.	13,400	13,463	11,999	8,900
Maize				
Bulgaria	882	1,506	1,505	1,425
Czechoslovakia	479	503	572	461
E. Germany	7	4	5	3
Hungary	2,833	3,558	3,504	2,705
Poland	34	19	47	33
Rumania	3,637	5,680	5,531	5,740
Total	7,872	11,270	11,164	10,367
U.S.S.R.	16,700	12,020	18,702	24,295
Total	24,572	23,290	29,866	34,662
Total Foodgrains				
E. Europe	40,952	47,837	47,305	46,449
U.S.S.R.	105,397	121,633	127,345	129,495
Total	146,349	169,470	174,650	175,944
Rice				
Bulgaria	45	29	32	36
Hungary	73	59	45	38
Rumania	37	55	49	31
Total	155	143	126	105
U.S.S.R.	216	214	187	240
Total	371	357	313	345

APPENDIX I: (Continued)
'000 tons

MEAT

	1958	1959	1960	1961
Bulgaria	288	301	278	323
Czechoslovakia	429	431	440[a]	445[a]
E. Germany	2,346	2,321	2,430	2,547
Hungary	248	586	573	601
Poland	1,778	1,698	1,737	1,899
Rumania	750[a]	800[a]	969	1,057
Total	5,839	6,137	6,427	6,872
U.S.S.R.	7,710	8,918	8,700	9,400
Total	13,549	15,055	15,127	16,272

DAIRY PRODUCTS

	1958	1959	1960	1961
Milk				
Bulgaria	987	1,030	1,114	1,189
Czechoslovakia	4,029	4,021	4,063	4,162
E. Germany	6,003	6,114	6,012	5,855
Hungary	1,951	1,989	1,955	1,898
Poland	11,863	12,306	12,488	12,759
Rumania	2,373	2,570	2,825	3,041
Total	27,206	28,060	28,457	28,904
U.S.S.R.	58,674	61,716	61,718	62,600
Total	85,880	89,776	90,275	91,504

APPENDIX I: (Continued)
'000 tons

DAIRY PRODUCTS: (Continued)

	1958	1959	1960	1961
Butter				
Bulgaria	6	8	11	11
Czechoslovakia	58	55	58	68
E. Germany	158	161	175	178
Hungary	17	17	17	16
Poland	162	170	167	167
Rumania	10	11	13	14
Total	411	422	441	454
U.S.S.R.	779	845	848	898
Total	1,190	1,267	1,289	1,352
Cheese				
Bulgaria	36	62	81	100
Czechoslovakia	70	75	75	80
E. Germany	34	35	37	39
Hungary	15	14	17	19
Poland	120	147	142	183
Rumania	37	36	34	41
Total	312	369	386	482
U.S.S.R.	239	244	268	270
Total	551	616	654	732
Eggs (million)				
Bulgaria	883	938	1,201	1,369
Czechoslovakia	2.070	2,135	2,267	2,351
E. Germany	3,027	3,127	3,512	3,602
Hungary	1,716	1,850	1,848	1,900
Poland	4,553	5,127	5,589	6,141
Rumania	2,002	2,160	2,355	2,600
Total	14,251	15,337	16,972	17,963
U.S.S.R.	22,400	24,500	27,464	29,309
Total	36,651	39,837	44,436	47,272

APPENDIX I: (Continued)
'000 tons

VEGETABLES

	1958	1959	1960	1961	1962
Sugar beet					
Bulgaria	882	1,450	1,650	1,463	1,300[a]
Czechoslovakia	6,491	4,609	7,853	6,000[a]	7,370[p]
E. Germany	6,976	4,659	6,837	4,657	...
Hungary	2,070	2,679	3,370	2,356	2,640[a]
Poland	8,427	5,975	10,262	11,555	11,120[a]
Rumania	1,732	3,446	3,399	2,911	...
Total	26,578	22,818	33,371	28,942	28,000[a]
USSR	54,400	43,942	57,728	50,911	48,900[a]
Total	80,978	66,760	91,099	79,853	76,900[a]
Potatoes					
Bulgaria	251	421	478	445	...
Czechoslovakia	6,589	6,334	5,093	5,331	7,130[p]
E. Germany	11,498	12,436	14,821	8,430	...
Hungary	2,600	2,366	2,656	1,630	1,880[a]
Poland	34,800	35,698	37,855	45,203	40,600[a]
Rumania	2,801	2,931	3,022	2,889	...
Total	58,539	60,186	63,925	63,928	...
USSR	86,500	86,561	84,374	84,310	68,900[a]
Total	145,039	146,747	148,299	148,238	...
Onions					
Bulgaria	88	120	120	95	
Czechoslovakia	57	70	67	60	
Hungary	40	95	68	57	
Poland	183	197	182	208	
Rumania	148	267	282	153	
Total	516	749	719	573	

APPENDIX I: (Continued)
'000 tons

VEGETABLES: (Continued)

	1958	1959	1960	1961
Tomatoes				
Bulgaria	464	479	634	726
Czechoslovakia	46	42	54	56
Hungary	151	196	202	199
Poland	244	218	164	200
Rumania	306	377	408	402
Total	1,211	1,312	1,462	1,583

EDIBLE PULSES

	1958	1959	1960	1961
Bulgaria	67	108	119	88
Czechoslovakia	23	28	34	36
E. Germany	52	34	65	70
Hungary	34	72	86	75
Poland	70	51	52	52
Rumania	127	153	251	241
Total	373	446	607	562
USSR[b]	818	986	1,270	2,180
Total	1,191	1,432	1,877	2,742

b, Figures for Dried Peas only.

APPENDIX I: (Continued)
'000 tons

FRUIT (Temperate)

	1958	1959	1960	1961
Bulgaria	1,347	1,346	1,120	1,325
Czechoslovakia	842	435	862	537
E. Germany	988	328	1,192	375
Hungary	1,439	1,185	1,003	1,528
Poland	845	450	1,113	616
Rumania	2,033	2,048	1,608	1,615
Total	7,494	5,792	6,698	5,996
USSR[b]	1,734	1,734	1,871	2,225
Total	9,228	7,526	8,769	8,221

b. Figures for Grapes only; an average of 30,000 tons a year of citrus was also produced.

SOYA BEANS

	1958	1959	1960	1961
Bulgaria	-	-	2	1
Hungary	1	1	2	1
Rumania	6	9	12	5
Total	7	10	16	7
USSR	229	224	225	220
Total	236	234	241	227

APPENDIX I: (Continued)
'000 tons

SUNFLOWER SEED

	1958	1959	1960	1961	1962
Bulgaria	221	279	344	301	350
Czechoslovakia	7	5	6	2	...
Hungary	100	115	68	105	130
Rumania	286	529	522	481	...
Total	614	928	840	889	...
USSR	4,626	3,019	3,967	4,753	...
Total	5,240	3,947	4,807	5,342	...

TEA

	1958	1959	1960	1961	1962
USSR	32	34	38	37	41[a]

a. Estimated. p. Plan estimate.

Source: FAO and national sources.

APPENDIX 2 - TRADE IN FOODSTUFFS

'000 tons

U.S.S.R.

Imports

	1958	1959	1960	1961
Wheat	323	247	98	656
Oats	31	9	3	-
Barley	176	1	22	-
Maize	262	-	117	23
Total cereals	792	257	240	679
Rice	501	689	501	20
Soya beans	1,446	2,193	2,861	2,181
Pulses	15	5	8	10
Sugar	395	335	1,717	3,597
Coffee	4	13	19	30
Cocoa beans	10	40	58	21
Tea	26	30	23	15
Meat, fresh	117	83	47	47
Meat, canned & prepared	34	27	17	11
Cattle, live ('000 head)	121	142	158	138
Pigs, live ('000 head)	58	55	55	300
Sheep, live ('000 head)	1,655	1,579	1,735	1,754
Butter	25	-	4	8
Cheese	-	3	-	-
Dried milk	-	-	3	2
Eggs (no. million)	373	110	113	161
Apples	155	144	151	108
Grapes	38	34	43	64
Oranges & tangerines	96	80	79[a]	65
Other citrus fruit	37	24	42[a]	36
Bananas	5	10	13	22
Raisins	28	22	16	11
Dates	5	5	9	25

a Including 17,000 tons reexported in each case.

APPENDIX 2 (Continued)
'000 tons

U. S. S. R. (Continued)

Exports

	1958	1959	1960	1961
Wheat	3,879	6,052	5,624	4,801
Oats	261	131	42	180
Barley	278	122	324	1,007
Maize	221	155	122	406
Rye	461	549	683	1,088
Total cereals	5,100	7,009	6,795	7,482
Rice	102	100	-	-
Sugar	218	214	264	951
Coffee	-	5	5	6
Cocoa beans	-	13	8	5
Tea	4	5	5	6
Meat, fresh	33	174	68	60
Meat, canned & prepared	1	1	6	6
Pigs, live ('000 head)	58	55	55	91
Butter	25	80	37	36
Cheese	-	1	3	4
Condensed milk	1	3	11	9

APPENDIX 2 (Continued)
'000 tons

BULGARIA

Imports

	1958	1959	1960	1961
Wheat	23	151	136	8
Oats	-	2	2	-
Barley	7	17	-	69
Rye	-	21	3	-
Maize	12	74	10	61
Total cereals	42	265	151	138
Rice	-	11	13	12
Soya beans	-	3	-	-
Sugar	-	31	37	106
Cocoa beans	1	1	1	1
Meat, fresh	-	1	15	5
Oranges & tangerines	3	4	2	1
Other citrus fruit	3	2	1	2

APPENDIX 2 (Continued)
'000 tons

BULGARIA (Continued)

Exports

	1958	1959	1960	1961
Wheat	6	11	33	10
Barley	7	-	-	4
Maize	36	6	137	104
Total cereals	49	17	170	118
Rice	10	9	8	5
Pulses	34	31	23	42
Sugar	23	15	39	74
Meat, fresh	22	22	21	21
of which pigmeat	19	16	14	13
Meat, prepared	8	7	11	11
Pigs, live ('000 head)	73	183	96	137
Butter	-	2	3	2
Cheese	1	5	6	7
Eggs (no. million)	280	204	436	534
Apples	19	33	36	39
Grapes	96	89	77	116
Pears	-	1	-	1
Potatoes	6	31	63	65
Onions	5	14	13	7

APPENDIX 2 (Continued)
'000 tons

CZECHOSLOVAKIA

Imports

	1958	1959	1960	1961
Wheat	965	1,639	1,486	1,127
Oats	5	-	-	-
Barley	93	13	64	110
Rye	60	158	191	182
Maize	193	95	261	118
Wheat flour	-	1	5	-
Total cereals	1,316	1,906	2,007	1,537
Rice	142	136	143	165
Soya beans	35	59	45	26
Pulses	3	14	8	12
Sugar	-	2	22	11
Coffee	5	8	8	14
Cocoa beans	10	12	13	15
Tea	2	1	1	1
Meat, fresh	66	103	106	82
Meat, canned & prepared	11	8	13	8
Cattle, live ('000 head)	-	4	-	7
Pigs, live ('000 head)	147	67	49	85
Butter	9	15	14	17
Cheese	1	-	1	1
Dried/condensed milk	-	-	3	1
Eggs (no. million)	57	54	70	74
Oranges & tangerines	17	23[a]	14	14
Other citrus fruit	16	19	20	24
Bananas	1	3	4	3
Apples	12	36	20	41
Grapes	28	22	25	19
Pears	1	2	1	-
Raisins	3	3	2	3
Potatoes	11	36	135	146
Onions	9	13	11	3

a Including 3,000 tons which were re-exported.

APPENDIX 2 (Continued)
'000 tons

CZECHOSLOVAKIA (Continued)

Exports

	1958	1959	1960	1961
Wheat	38	77	48	16
Barley	32	27	25	29
Rye	5	1	-	-
Maize	-	-	6	-
Total cereals	75	105	79	45
Rice	68	57	-	2
Sugar	401	392	319	720
Meat, fresh	1	2	1	2
Meat canned & prepared	2	3	1	3
Butter	2	1	-	-
Cheese	2	2	2	3
Eggs (no. million)	100	111	101	154
Apples	2	3	1	-
Pears	7	4	5	3
Potatoes	19	23	13	8
Onions	2	16	13	7

APPENDIX 2 (Continued)
'000 tons

EAST GERMANY

Imports

	1958	1959	1960	1961
Wheat	1,292	1,335	1,520	1,250
Oats	133	63	58	124
Barley	85	83	116	128
Rye	207	207	234	245
Maize	143	149	151	177
Total cereals	1,860	1,837	2,079	1,924
Rice	59	115	143	30
Pulses	13	9	2	2
Sugar	-	-	62	112
Coffee	16	23	23	21
Cocoa beans	9	15	12	13
Tea	2	2	1	1
Meat,fresh	63	193	104	108
Cattle, live ('000 head)	18	13	8	1
Pigs, live ('000 head)	-	1	-	100
Butter	22	69	44	51
Cheese	12	15	20	21
Eggs (no. million)	101	117	57	21
Oranges & tangerines	10	16	8	11
Other citrus fruit	11	16	5	14
Apples	29	47	16	19
Grapes	30	35	19	15
Pears	5	2	-	1
Raisins	19	7	8	6
Dates	1	7	6	2
Potatoes	31	44	55	90
Onions	26	9	11	10

APPENDIX 2 (Continued)
'000 tons

EAST GERMANY (Continued)

Exports

	1958	1959	1960	1961
Wheat	1	18	-	3
Sugar	182	357	139	411
Meat, fresh	27	3	6	2
Cattle, live ('000 head)	-	1	1	-
Pigs, live ('000 head)	5	2	7	-
Eggs (no. million)	35	28	14	1
Potatoes	6	24	3	1
Onions	-	1	-	1

APPENDIX 2 (Continued)
'000 tons

HUNGARY

Imports

	1958	1959	1960	1961
Wheat	101	256	323	508
Wheat flour	-	3	33	34
Oats	-	-	-	2
Barley	78	3	1	64
Rye	-	17	-	19
Maize	14	55	41	120
Total cereals	193	334	398	747
Rice	15	30	18	22
Soya beans	53	62	57	17
Pulses	-	3	7	1
Sugar	52	11	30	-
Coffee	1	6	3	3
Cocoa beans	2	4	4	3
Tea	-	1	1	-
Meat, fresh	4	11	25	20
Pigs, live ('000 head)	4	-	-	21
Butter	-	-	2	2
Dried/condensed milk	-	-	1	2
Eggs (no. million)	-	9	-	3
Apples	-	-	-	1
Oranges & tangerines	4	7	6	6
Other citrus fruit	11	13	13	12
Raisins	-	-	3	3
Potatoes	1	25	10	34
Onions	4	2	-	-

APPENDIX 2 (Continued)
'000 tons

HUNGARY (Continued)

Exports

	1958	1959	1960	1961
Wheat	57	53	24	94
Wheat flour	7	9	30	17
Barley	1	7	1	27
Maize	43	46	38	54
Total cereals	108	115	93	192
Rice	49	25	14	3
Pulses	29	28	40	32
Sugar	30	68	147	119
Meat, fresh	28	38	35	43
of which pigmeat	7	9	14	6
poultry meat	14	16	15	18
Meat, canned & prepared	9	10	1	1
Cattle, live ('000 head)	91	93	123	92
Pigs, live ('000 head)	141	135	105	78
Butter	7	5	6	4
Cheese	4	6	6	8
Eggs (no. million)	148	163	118	135
Apples	27	64	23	78
Grapes	22	15	9	23
Pears	1	1	-	1
Potatoes	49	38	66	70
Onions	15	29	25	10

APPENDIX 2 (Continued)
'000 tons

POLAND

Imports

	1958	1959	1960	1961
Wheat	666	1,313	1,700	1,739
Wheat flour	-	-	-	14
Barley	173	372	231	317
Rye	210	2	109	313
Maize	56	13	46	51
Total cereals	1,105	1,700	2,086	2,434
Rice	28	102	100	60
Soya beans	46	48	42	23
Pulses	-	-	-	1
Sugar	-	45	154	261
Coffee	2	8	4	4
Cocoa beans	9	8	11	10
Tea	3	6	3	2
Meat, fresh	15	42	12	7
Meat, canned & prepared	1	4	6	2
Butter	-	-	-	-
Cheese	-	1	1	1
Dried / condensed milk	5	5	1	8
Oranges & tangerines	14	24	10	12
Other citrus fruit	21	28	22	24
Apples	-	1	-	2
Grapes	16	15	12	13
Raisins	-	1	1	1
Dates	-	1	1	-
Potatoes	-	-	1	2

APPENDIX 2 (Continued)
'000 tons

POLAND (Continued)

Exports

	1958	1959	1960	1961
Wheat flour	-	1	-	-
Barley	59	31	82	103
Total cereals	59	32	82	103
Pulses	4	2	1	4
Meat, fresh	14	17	26	83
of which poultry meat	12	15	14	19
pigmeat	1	-	2	32
Meat, canned & prepared	77	82	84	87
of which bacon	48	51	48	49
Cattle, live ('000 head)	3	11	46	22
Pigs, live ('000 head)	439	372	339	665
Butter	24	23	29	27
Cheese	2	5	6	4
Dried/condensed milk	-	-	-	1
Casein	...	...	13	9
Eggs (no million)	445	738	972	1,443
Apples	32	10	20	13
Pears	1	-	1	-
Potatoes	91	183	75	163
Onions	9	41	23	29

APPENDIX 2 (Continued)
'000 tons

RUMANIA

Imports

	1958	1959	1960	1961
Wheat	193	6	101	-
Oats	-	5	-	-
Maize	8	1	1	1
Total cereals	201	12	102	1
Rice	3	-	14	-
Soya beans	-	2	1	-
Pulses	-	2	3	3
Sugar	43	31	-	33
Coffee	-	-	1	-
Cocoa beans	-	1	1	1
Meat, fresh	1	-	3	4
Cattle, live ('000 head)	-	-	2	2
Pigs, live ('000 head)	-	-	-	-
Cheese	-	-	1	-
Eggs (no. million)	-	18	17	24
Oranges & tangerines	3	3	5	5
Other citrus fruit	1	7	6	8
Potatoes	-	-	-	1
Onions	1	1	-	2

APPENDIX 2 (Continued)
'000 tons

RUMANIA (Continued)

Exports

	1958	1959	1960	1961
Wheat	23	-	35	8
Oats	-	2	-	-
Barley	1	1	-	-
Rye	-	3	24	43
Maize	429	60	291	626
Total cereals	453	66	350	677
Pulses	26	4	2	3
Sugar	1	-	83	160
Meat, fresh	3	6	24	12
Meat, canned & prepared	-	2	2	1
Cattle, live ('000 head)	1	1	16	6
Pigs, live ('000 head)	1	9	37	22
Butter	-	1	1	1
Cheese	-	-	-	1
Eggs (no. million)	47	46	101	106
Apples	-	9	4	9
Grapes	20	23	17	18
Potatoes	-	4	-	-

Notes: - Denotes less than 500 tons. ... Not available.

Sources FAO and national statistics.